T0354416

WALKING THROUGH WIDOWHOOD

A WOMAN'S JOURNEY FROM DIAGNOSIS OF HER HUSBAND'S CANCER THROUGH DEATH AND BEYOND

Patricia McQuarrie

WESTBOW
PRESS®
A DIVISION OF THOMAS NELSON
& ZONDERVAN

WestBow Press books may be ordered through booksellers or by contacting:

WestBow Press
A Division of Thomas Nelson & Zondervan
1663 Liberty Drive
Bloomington, IN 47403
www.westbowpress.com
1 (866) 928-1240

ISBN: 978-1-9736-1647-4 (sc)
ISBN: 978-1-9736-1648-1 (hc)
ISBN: 978-1-9736-1646-7 (e)

Library of Congress Control Number: 2018901013

Print information available on the last page.

WestBow Press rev. date: 06/05/2018

INTRODUCTION

Tﾟhis book is about my husband Bob and our journey together from the time we met until Bob's death. It is about how God can take two confused and broken young people and transform them into happy, well functioning adults who, after thirty years together, ended their journey loving each other and their Lord Jesus Christ. It is a tribute to my dear husband. Bob, if I had not met and fallen in love with you I would not be the person I am today. Knowing, and being married to you, has blessed my life. Among a host of other things, you taught me how to die with dignity. I look forward to meeting you again one day.

It is not my intent to be dishonoring to my children or the memory of my late husband in any way, but in order to complete the story I had to tell the bad with the good. I pray my children will understand. My intent is to relate facts and truths, to show the Glory and Power of God. If He can change us, and He did, He can change anyone. Glory be to God!

DEDICATION

To my Children: Clay, Patti, Jennie and Michael who sacrificially helped their dad and I through this journey. Words cannot express the depth of my love and gratitude to you.

SPECIAL THANKS

To my Lord Jesus Christ, who planted the seed in my heart and gave me the title of this book *Walking Through Widowhood* so many years ago.

To my friend Bev Allen, who encouraged me to keep a journal once Bob was diagnosed with cancer. I thought,"Who would want to journal this" but I did it anyway. Without my four- year daily journal, this book would not have been written. Thank you, Bev!

Special thanks also to my good friend Jeri Stevenson: Licensed Minister, Prayer Counselor, and founder of Pacific Hope Ministries in Lynden, Washington. All the hours of wisdom and expertise you gave me helped with transcribing from my journal to book form. Both your belief in this book and encouragement, kept me going at times when I felt like giving up. Thank you my friend!

Thanks to my long- time friend Jennifer Whitney Clements: Writer, Producer, and founder of Word Garden Productions. Your help was invaluable to me, I will be forever grateful!

Thanks to Mary Dickson for proof reading and advising me.

Thanks also to Cristy Watson for the final editing of my book.

To my many friends and family, you know who you are, you were there for us, comforting and encouraging us every step of the way. Thank you!

CHAPTER 1

Y ou are going to become a widow! Those words were
so clear and matter of fact, I shocked. No! No! It can't
be true.

My husband Bob and I were sitting in the den watching
sports on TV, not being a sports fan I was bored and restless.
After working all day, Bob enjoyed watching sports and
since I loved being with him, that was how we spent most
of our evenings.

It was one evening in February, 1985, I was talking to the
Lord and feeling resentful over all the hours we wasted in
front of the TV. I remember asking the Lord, "Is this the life
you want for me? " I was forty-five years old, our children,
Clay, Patti, Jennie and Michael were grown and had left
home by this time, making Bob and I empty nesters.

In many ways I loved our time alone but at other times
I felt as though my life was slipping away. I prayed, "Lord,
you know how I want to serve you; I would love to have a
woman's ministry, but how can I teach women anything
when I struggle in so many areas myself? You know Lord,

one of my biggest struggles is not loving my husband the way I know you want me to love him."

The voice came again, stronger and more clearly, "You are going to become a widow." I knew it came from outside myself. The voice had authority, as well as gentleness. Could God be speaking to me? No, it couldn't be! I felt calm, and had no fear during this whole experience, I just felt numb.

I looked over at Bob. He was so handsome and had never felt better in his life. It was true he had been in the hospital in early January, for what we thought was a bleeding ulcer. Clay, our oldest son had come home from California for Christmas that year. Bob was sick and looked terrible. We thought he had the flu so we took him to the Doctors office. Upon arrival, he immediately collapsed. The paramedics were called and Bob was rushed to the hospital where it was discovered he had a bleeding ulcer. Bob told the Doctors he had been losing blood for a long time so he received several blood transfusions after which he looked and felt great.

It took me some time to agree with the words I heard in the den, you are going to become a widow. Finally I thought, "OK, statistics show that women do live longer than men. It's probably true that I will become a widow one day."

I soon forgot hearing that I would become a widow. However, sometime later, that statement would return to me. It was at that time I realized God wanted me to hear those words. He did not want me to be paralyzed with fear for what was about to come. For the time being, He removed those words from my memory.

CHAPTER 2

As I looked back over our life together, I realized we had not always felt love for each other. Bob and I met in May 1958, when I was eighteen and he was twenty four years old. A mutual friend took me to meet him in downtown, Vancouver, B.C., where he worked pumping gas at a car dealership. When he came out to fill our car with gas I was attracted to him immediately: he was very good looking, and had a quick, easy smile that made my eighteen year old knees go weak. I thought he was cute, but way too young for me. Later, I found out he was older than me by six years. As we got to know each other and talked about it we both had a good laugh. I loved that when he smiled his eyes seemed to disappear.

I could tell by our short conversation he had a great sense of humor. It seemed he was attracted to me as well, as he soon called and we began seeing each other. After dating three months, we became engaged and were married a year later, on August 14, 1959.

Our Wedding day photo highlights the best of our times together. However, even from the beginning, our relationship was difficult. During the year of our engagement, Bob seemed to prefer spending more time with his drinking buddies than with me. I resented his treatment of me and did not hesitate to tell him. If we had been more mature we would have known we were not ready for marriage.

Bob was an only child from a broken home. He felt his mother was possessive and domineering, which was annoying to him. I came from an extremely abusive home where I was told repeatedly that I was stupid and should never have been born. Being only eighteen years old I remember thinking; "If I met a man and got married he would love me as I had never been loved and we would live happily ever after." I felt that once I was married my needs would be met and I would be happy. What I did not realize was that no human being can fill the emptiness in our hearts, only God can do that. Both our childhoods were chaotic and void of any emotional security. We were two, deeply wounded, and broken young adults that had never grown up. Bob's attitude was that no woman was going to tell him what to do and my attitude was that no man was going to tell me what to do. Both of our attitudes were subconscious and we were not aware of them but they persisted none the less. What a perfect recipe for disaster!!

What I saw in Bob as fun loving, carefree and charming turned out to be, in my eyes, irresponsible and insensitive. What he saw in me as sensitive and responsible, turned out to be in his eyes, insecure, needy, and over responsible; controlling, I think he would call it!! However, even throughout our struggles we were blessed with a good sense of humor that helped us get through those hard times. As I look back, I am so glad that Bob was my husband. Because of the pain and struggles we endured, I gave my life to God and met Jesus Christ as my Saviour.

When our oldest son Clay was two years old and Patti was a baby, we moved from Vancouver, B.C., to Bellingham, Washington in the United States. I was so glad to move away from his drinking buddies, and hoped things would be better for us.

By the time I was twenty six we had four children under six years old, Clay, Patti, Jennie and Michael. My babies were the light of my life, but because of the tension between

Bob and me, I soon became overwhelmed. It was a stressful time for both of us. Bob's way of dealing with stress was to spend time drinking with his friends, making my life even more stressful. Three or four nights a week he would not call to tell me he was not coming home after work. I would prepare dinner, only to have him arrive at two am. When we lived in B.C., I always knew he would be home by twelve-thirty am, when the beer parlors closed. After we moved to Bellingham, the first night he went out after work with his new found drinking partners, he did not come home till after two am. I was beside myself with worry and anger. He looked at me with a big smile and said, "The taverns don't close till 2:00 am here," like it was the most wonderful news in the world. Bob was flirtatious when he was drinking and this behavior was also distressing. Many times he would not come home until morning, and often with lipstick all over his collar. He had told me early in our marriage that he didn't believe men were designed to be with only one woman for the rest of their lives; they just were not made that way. As a young woman, and new bride, I was devastated. Consequently my anxiety level went through the roof when he was out until the wee hours, as I believed he would not resist temptation if it came. He truly believed he did not need to be faithful to me.

I was overwhelmed with pain and jealousy. He would arrive home apologetic, vowing he would never again stay out all night. I loved him and wanted to believe him, but it happened over and over again. Many of my friends wondered why I put up with his hurtful behavior, but there was a part of me that was in total denial. All he had to do was flash that winning smile and I would melt. He had me wrapped around his little finger and he knew it. For me, it was almost like an addiction.

Several times I took the kids and left for a few days but I was in such pain without him, I always went back. I was hooked, and didn't know how to break free. I vacillated from being filled with love for him one minute, and hating him the next. This continued to be the pattern of our relationship for the first ten years of our marriage.

Neither one of us had any idea how to love each other, let alone, how to communicate. I tried for years to get Bob to go with me for counseling, but to no avail. He didn't believe in counseling, so I was left to go on my own. I was in counseling for years. Unfortunately I was such a nervous wreck by the time I finally went, the counselor and I were only putting band-aids on the latest crisis; never getting to the root of our problems. Eventually, on the threat of my leaving, Bob consented to come with me for counseling so they could straighten *me* out, since according to him, *I* was the one with the problem. The counselor explained that Bob was happy enough with the way things were, as he was doing whatever he wanted so in his world everything was fine, however, I was filled with hurt and anger which was unnoticed by him. Our sessions with the counselor didn't last very long. Bob would not say anything so I had to do most of the talking. The counselor asked Bob if he felt he couldn't share his heart with me, or if he just didn't want to?. When Bob replied that he did not want to share his heart with me, I was devastated and felt hopeless. The counselor finally said if Bob was not going to look at himself there was no point in coming back. So we never went back. I remember the counselor telling us it would be a miracle if our marriage made it because our needs were so different. I continued to go for counseling by myself and spent twenty years in and out of counseling during our thirty year marriage. Without the help I received we never would have stayed together.

Often, after a late night of drinking and carousing, the next morning Bob would say: "Come on hon, I won't do it again. Now let's not ruin today". I finally learned we were never going to talk about our issues and nothing would ever be resolved, so I stuffed my feelings down and tried not to *"ruin today"*. But my feelings were building up, like a volcano inside me.

My heart was breaking while my body was reacting to the stress. I suffered from Post Partum depression after my last child was born; I had a nervous breakdown and was under a doctor's care for many years. At one point, I saw a lawyer about a legal separation but could not go through with it, because I could not bear to go to work and leave my children with babysitters. I was not emotionally healthy enough to have financial responsibility for my children. In those days, going on welfare was not an option, at least for me, it wasn't. I was able to take good physical care of my children, but unfortunately I had nothing left when it came to meeting their emotional needs. I was so close to tears all the time, that when they cried, I usually cried along with them. In truth, I was not able to nurture them as I should have, and because of that they suffered. Later when I was getting emotionally healthy, I spent many years beating myself up about this, suffering guilt and shame for not being able to be the mother I needed to be for them. It is my prayer that my children will forgive me for the mistakes I made while raising them.

CHAPTER 3

By this time the children were all in school. A friend asked me to go with her to a Bible study class. I was nervous about it and we laughed when she said it was for neurotic women; we both agreed I qualified!!

I had never been to church or Sunday school when I was growing up and had a real fear of church people. I thought you had to talk about Holy things and I did not know any Holy things to talk about. I did not want my children to have the same fear about church as I had, so we began attending a neighborhood church when our youngest child, Michael, was a baby.

Even though we had been going to church off and on for a couple of years, this was my first exposure to Bible study, so it was all new. We studied the Book of John that whole year. I believed in God but knew very little about Jesus, and the Book of John, is all about Jesus. When I was asked what I thought about a passage I would go blank, like Bambi in the headlights and say "I don't know." I could not articulate what it meant to me, but I was gleaning a lot just being there, listening to what others were saying. I have since learned that when someone is in a group and doesn't participate it does not mean they are not receiving from the Lord.

At the end of that year, the group decided to go to a woman's retreat at the Warm Beach Conference Center, in Washington State. I had only recently heard the word "retreat" from a Catholic friend and I thought they must be for 'super religious' people. I asked the leader if she thought I could bluff my way through the retreat. She said 'yes' and that the only time I might be uncomfortable is when we got into a small group to pray. She added that they may go around the room and ask for a short, one sentence prayer from each of us; maybe something for which we were thankful. I had never prayed out loud before, so I was terrified. I remember thinking, "what will I pray?" I finally came up with: "Thank you Lord, that I was born in a free country." I mean really, I could have been born in a communist country right?

So I practiced that sentence over and over and sure enough, at the retreat we went around the room in our little prayer circle with each one of us taking our turn to pray. By the time it was my turn, my heart was pounding, my palms were sweating and I could hardly breathe. I managed to muster up all my courage and get my sentence prayer out. "Thank you Lord, that I was born in a free country." What a relief! I did it! I was so proud of myself.

The speaker was wonderful. Do you remember the old TV series 'Ma and Pa' Kettle from the late 1950's? They had a simple, down - home type of humor. I felt like I was looking at and listening to, Ma Kettle. Like Ma Kettle, she wore her hair in a bun and had the same type of accent and spoke with lots of humor. Among other things she said, "If you died tonight, would you know for sure you are going to heaven? If not, you had better talk to the Lord about it when you go to bed." So I did. Even though we had been going to church for some time I did not know I could interact with God on a personal level. So I said, "I am going to be with you when I die, aren't I? I love you Lord, so I give you my life. Please use me for your purpose." When I woke up the next morning something felt different; I had a deep joy inside of me that I had not had before. I did not recognize what had happened to me for several months but finally came to realize I now had the Holy Spirit living within me; now my relationship with God and Jesus was personal. The Bible says in Romans 8 verse 11 KJV "But if the spirit of him that raised up Jesus from the dead dwell in you, he that raised up Christ from the dead shall also quicken your mortal bodies because of his spirit that dwelleth in you." I knew my body had new life because I felt so happy and much more content. I was twenty nine years old and have since, continued to grow in my relationship with the Lord.

At that time I was on a very high dose of tranquilizers. I felt guilty about that and felt now that I knew Christ, I should not need medication any more. So I quit cold turkey without consulting my Doctor. That was a potentially dangerous thing to do, and it took me months to recover. But slowly, I began to feel better. As I look back, I can see the Lord protected my health as I was stopping my medication.

CHAPTER 4

As the years went on, I continued to pray and ask God to change Bob. Finally, I felt the Lord was saying "No honey, you don't get it. It's YOU I want to change." I was the one who wanted things to change so I had to be willing to change first. I remember asking God if I was doing something that may have been preventing Bob from coming to the Lord. I had been praying for ten years for Bob to accept the Lord as his savior, but it seemed like it was taking so long for him to respond. God revealed to me I needed to forgive my father for abusing me before I was free to fully love my husband, my attitude was preventing Bob from fully responding to God's love. Because my father had severely abused me as a child I had pulled into myself and not been able to express my emotions. My feelings were stuffed and hidden deep within my heart. I was inwardly angry and hateful towards my father and those emotions were directed onto my husband, as I felt mistreated by him, as well, Ephesians 4:31,32 NIV says; "Get rid of all bitterness, rage and anger, be kind and compassionate to one another, forgiving each other just as in Christ, God forgave you." God desires that we look into our own hearts to see the part we play in our relationships, as we can only change ourselves, and not another. By holding on to those past hurts I was only hurting myself, and my marriage. After much prayer, and with the help of a Christian counselor, I reached the point where I could say, "Dad I forgive you for" and then I listed each offence God brought to my memory. I remember the peace that flooded my heart when I made the decision to forgive my father. God had changed my heart, even though I was not immediately aware of the change. The Bible says in Ezekiel 36:26: KJV "A new heart also I will give you, and a new spirit I will put within you: and I will take away the stony heart out of your flesh, and I will give you a heart of flesh." God began to show me how my behavior was causing problems in my marriage. Because I was so filled with anger at Bob for cheating on me, shutting me out of his life, and making me feel unimportant, I behaved selfishly and tried to put myself first. One morning I was making breakfast for him before he went to work, I was cutting the grapefruit, and knowing that one half of the grapefruit is sweeter than the other, I put the stem end, which is not as sweet and juicy as the other end, on Bob's plate. The Lord showed me I usually kept the best for myself. I was so embarrassed! Even though it was only God and I that knew what was going on, I felt exposed. I could not believe my behavior. I thanked God for showing me what I had been doing, and immediately switched our plates. Whenever I thought of leaving during this time I remembered the verse that talked about God's grace being sufficient for me. If I left I would be telling God His grace was not sufficient for me and I would be telling the world the same. I knew God would see me through the hard times if I let Him. I needed to learn to love my husband without expecting anything in return. Would that be easy? No. Would it come naturally? No. Was it possible? Yes. If I let Jesus love overflow from me to Bob it would be Agape love, the love that God has for us. He loves us for who we are not for how we behave. I had to learn to love Bob as God loves us.

As God continued to show me how to better love my husband our relationship began to change. He came home after work to be with family. He always had a drink or two before dinner, but at least he was home. I loved that! He still had his golf night every Wednesday and did not get home till 2.00 am, but it was only one night a week now, so I was grateful. Matthew 7:12 NIV says "So in everything, do to others what you would have them do to you, for this sums up the law and the prophets." I learned that love begets love. As a married man Bob's behavior was not acceptable but my attitude towards him was not acceptable for healing our relationship and as I showed love to Bob, he began to respond and love me back.

One evening, Bob and I were hit by a drunk driver and our car was thrown deep into a ditch. When the paramedics came I heard Bob say, "I'm ok. It's my wife. Take care of my wife." He kept repeating, *"my wife, my wife"*, over and over, with desperate concern in his voice. I remember feeling shock, as I had never in all the years of our marriage felt that Bob loved me. I realized that when he was growing up, he did not feel loved, therefore he was unable to show love to those closest to him. I remember thinking, he really does love me! I felt joy and love for Bob flood over me as I heard his concern for me.

I was a Christian for ten years before Bob accepted Christ. He did it in his usual quiet way and it was three months before he even told me, saying, "And don't you tell anyone"! I had been praying for so long and I was so excited, it was hard not to tell the world. I knew he was not ready to have his buddies know, and my Christian friends would make such a fuss over him it would make him uncomfortable. It was not my place to tell anyone about his decision and I knew he would share this news when he was ready.

Occasionally we went to a Christian counseling organization in Seattle, called Burden Bearers, where we worked on our family issues. The counselor said we needed to spend more time together as a couple suggesting we go away for a weekend, just the two of us. I loved that news!! Our anniversary was August 14, and that following year Bob ordered flowers and had them delivered to our door. He also wrote on my card to be ready at 5:30 and to wear something nice, as we were going out. After work he picked me up and took me to a lovely restaurant for dinner. What a wonderful surprise. My birthday was January 2, and he continued to surprise me by making special plans. I felt new hope rising up within me.

It seemed Bob appreciated my reaction, as the next August he picked me up from my part time job and said we are going away for the weekend. I said, "I can't because I have to work tomorrow." He replied, "no you don't, I took care of that too." He had arranged for a babysitter, packed my bag for me and off we went. He would not tell me where we were going, and all I knew was that we were heading north. The excitement in me kept building, and we were halfway there before, I realized we were going to Harrison Hot Springs Resort, in B.C. That was one of the most special times of my life, and certainly in our marriage, I felt so loved and cherished. He too felt good about it because he shared the same surprise (not the same place) with me twice a year, every August for our anniversary and every January for my birthday until the day he died. He never told me where we were going: just what time to be ready, what to pack, and we started out. If we went North on the freeway, I knew we were going to the Vancouver area, and if South, the Seattle area. That would be all I would know. Those times were pivotal in reconnecting our relationship and renewing our love for each other. I was so pleased that God showed me, by looking at my actions, I understood how they were negatively affecting our marriage. As I changed my behavior, by learning how to love my husband unconditionally, our relationship changed for the better and now it was flourishing. I wish I had known this earlier in my life, but I was grateful for the years ahead.

There were so many funny and unusual circumstances that happened over the years I am surprised Bob did not give up. He would have flowers delivered to the house, and when they came, I was usually out. It got to the point, where he would ask, with irritation in his voice, what my plans were for the next day. He really wanted to surprise me and I was not cooperating. After a few years, I finally caught on (quick learner eh?). We always had a good laugh over his surprises that didn't seem to work out.

We both loved to swim at the hotels where we stayed. I'll never forget the time in Seattle, when we got all settled in our room, changed into our swimsuits, and headed down to the pool, only to find it was closed for repairs. Bob had chosen that hotel so carefully simply because of the pool.

In 1983, we had gone in to Vancouver early so we would be at the hotel for New Year's Eve. We went to bed early, as there was a full day of football the next day that Bob wanted to watch. We were dead asleep when the fire alarm went off at midnight. All the guests went to the hotel lobby in our night attire, mingling around with each other until they discovered it was a false alarm. The management brought in food and drinks for us and gave us a free night's lodging. That's how we spent that New Year's Eve!

The last time Bob planned a surprise trip, he made reservations at the Laurel Point Inn in Victoria, B.C. The ferries were late and we got there around 7.00 pm. In those days, there were no cell phones so we could not tell them we would be late. When we got to the hotel to check in, the desk clerk said,"You have already been checked in Mr. McQuarrie. Bob said "That can't be, we have just arrived." After further investigating, they discovered that another man with the name McQuarrie had checked in, and was given our room. What are the chances of that? Bob said, "I suppose you gave them the fruit basket I ordered too?" They were apologetic and arranged to put us up at another hotel, in downtown Victoria. They said it had just been remodeled and was lovely, and asked us to please come back the next day and they would have our suite ready for us.

When we parked our car and were walking to the hotel,

even though I was on Bob's arm, we were followed, and Bob was propositioned by a beautiful, albeit, scantily dressed woman. We discovered that the hotel had been used by prostitutes and had been shut down so they could remodel and change it's former image. The hotel had just reopened and it was lovely, even though the clientele had not seemed to have received the memo. We laughed about that for a long time to come, joking about spending our anniversary in a brothel.

The next day we went back to the original hotel, and they showed us to our suite where they soon delivered a large fruit basket, along with a bottle of champagne.

FACING DEATH

"Do not be afraid for I am with
you and will Bless you".

Gen 26:24 The Living Bible

CHAPTER 5

I am glad this wisdom came when it did. We would need to be strong in our relationship, because it was about to be tested again!

God provided a wonderful caring doctor, who walked very closely with us during our painful journey. In March 1985, Bob went back to see the doctor for a recheck of what we thought might be his ulcer. He was still losing blood, so he was sent for more extensive tests. A tumor was found in his colon. 'A tumor,- no way. This can't be, Bob was only fifty years old.

He later told me that for the last year he had been coming home from work to use the bathroom because he was so weak he would have to lay down afterward until he got his strength back. He knew he had been losing blood but did not tell anyone. I could not believe it. It was so like Bob to keep things to himself. Once again, I felt like my world was coming to an end. I walked through that time like a robot, just doing what needed to be done but not feeling much of anything. Neither of us knew what we were facing.

There were more tests, more doctor visits, and more

waiting for results. Finally the dreaded phone call from the doctor came. I answered the phone so I was the first to hear the tumor was malignant!! Shock and numbness set in. I could not believe it and yet, it was true. I felt such a deep sorrow come over me as I handed the phone to Bob. While he talked to the doctor, I wondered how he would be able to handle the news. Cold fear gripped my heart. What if Bob dies? Oh, no, I can't allow myself to think that way. We have to have hope, (I had forgotten the words I heard in the den that night). The Lord knew this was going to happen to us and I knew he cared for us. Once I let those thoughts in, I was able to feel God's comfort. I went to Bob after he hung up the phone, threw my arms around him, and said how sorry I was. We held each other tight for a long time, drawing comfort from each other.

The part I dreaded the most was telling our adult children. I knew they would be shocked and devastated. We had never known how to share our feelings with each other as a family. Now, I would have to watch them suffer and not know how to comfort them.

Michael was nineteen, Jennie twenty- one, Patti twenty-three and Clay- twenty five. None of them were living at home at this time. Clay was living in California, Patti had just returned from a season of fishing in Alaska and was living in Seattle, Jennie was working in Portland, and Mike was working in Bellingham. As each one of our children came to visit, we told them the painful and shocking news. We cried and hugged trying to be brave and reassure each other that God had His hand in all of what was happening and we needed to trust Him. Because Clay was in California, he had to be told over the telephone. He decided to quit his job and move back home to be near his family. Michael flew to California to help Clay drive the U-haul back to Washington. It was encouraging for Bob and I to see our children pulling together and supporting us.

A few years earlier, Bob had realized his dream, to own his own business and he opened an auto parts store. He also installed air conditioning and cruise control in automobiles for the local dealerships. In those days they were not put on at the factory so had to be installed by private companies. We were doing fairly well and then in the mid 1970's the bottom fell out of the auto industry. Many new car dealerships went out of business and consequently we lost our business as well. We had a beautiful 5 bedroom home in the Fairhaven area overlooking Bellingham Bay. It was tied into our business loan so we ended up losing our home as well as our business. We moved into a little rental house and Bob went to work as parts manager for the Bellingham Honda dealership. That was extremely hard on Bob, as he felt like he had lost everything he had worked so hard for in the last twenty-five years. This news concerning his health was another devastating blow for him to deal with.

On March 26, 1985, Bob and I went to see the surgeon who would perform the operation. He explained that he would take out part of the bowel then reconnect it. The tumor was in a position on the bowel where they did not think a colostomy bag would be needed. Praise the Lord! Bob had such a look of relief on his face. Both doctors were not anticipating any problems and were hopeful that if the tumor had not broken through the wall of the colon, it should be a successful surgery and Bob shouldn't have any further problems. They would not know for sure until they did the surgery but at this point the outlook was good. We left the office feeling hopeful, and I thanked the Lord! Surgery was scheduled for April 1, 1985.

As we looked back over the last few days and weeks, at all the fears and tears, we experienced a oneness that we had never known before. We held each other close as we cried together for the first time in our twenty-six years of marriage. We drew strength and comfort from the Lord, as well as each other.

As I look back, I think of all the years we spent fighting instead of pulling together. Bob said "I think I needed this experience to bring me closer to the Lord." He had been coming to church with the kids and I, on and off for the last several years and when things became tense between us, he would say, "I think I need to come back to church "and he would. Each time he returned to church it made a difference in how we interacted with each other, which was a great comfort for all of us.

CHAPTER 6

On Sunday, March 31, 1985, Bob was admitted to the hospital for surgery. After he was settled I went home to bed and lay awake for a long time. My mind was racing and I couldn't relax. "What if they didn't get all the cancer?" I still had not remembered the voice I heard in the den that night long ago. I could picture the doctor telling me it was worse than they thought. "Are you trying to prepare me Lord, or am I just torturing myself?"

I must not be fearful. Philippians 4:8 in the KJV Bible says, "Finally brethren, whatsoever things are true, whatsoever things are honest, whatsoever things are just, whatsoever things are pure, whatsoever things are lovely, whatsoever things are of good report; if there be any virtue, and if there be any praise, think on these things." I knew I had to focus on the Lord or I would not be able to go through this terrifying time. I forced myself to let go, and finally fell asleep.

On Monday, April 1st, 1985, the thought crossed my mind. "Is this an April fool's joke? Is this really happening ?" It all seemed so surreal. I went to the hospital early to be with Bob. Our pastor came and we prayed with Bob before the nurses took him to surgery. I walked beside him, holding his hand as they wheeled him down the hall. I remember thinking "Well Lord, Bob is in your hands now." I could feel the prayers of the friends who were praying for us, and this gave me great comfort and peace.

It seemed no time at all before the nurse came and called me into the consultation room. As soon as I saw the look on the doctor's face, I knew it was not good news. He said they had taken 2.5 feet of Bob's colon, but the tumor had spread from the colon wall to the liver. There were spots on the upper left, and lower right, area of the liver and they could not be removed. They cauterized both spots but felt they would continue to spread and there would be a re occurrence. As soon as the doctor shared this, I remembered the words from that night so long ago "YOU ARE GOING TO BECOME A WIDOW."

My heart felt like it had stopped beating. "Oh dear God, NO!!" I felt completely numb, like I was watching a movie, but was not really in it. At the same time, I felt a strange sensation of being comforted. God really did know and care about us. He had warned me ahead of time. He wanted me to know he would be walking through this whole journey with us, and that thought brought peace in the midst of sorrow.

I stayed with Bob in the hospital room as he came in and out of the anesthetic. I was so worried about how he would take the news. The first time Bob came out of the anesthetic, he asked me, "How did it go?" I said it went well, as the surgery did go well but the outcome was not good. At this point, I did not think it would be wise to tell him the whole truth. The next time he came out of the anesthetic, he asked me if they got all the cancer. My heart sank. I did not want to cause him any distress because he was not fully awake but he was alert enough to recognize if I was not being honest with him; I knew that would hurt him more. I told him about the two spots on the liver, but they had cauterized them, and not to worry. That seemed to satisfy him.

I left the hospital about dinnertime, completely exhausted. When I got home Mike was there so I told him about the outcome of the surgery. We hugged each other and cried. We reassured each other that the Lord knew how badly we were all hurting and that He was still in control.

What a comfort to be able to talk with Mike and share the Lord. Even though our children were on their own journey, they were all Christians, and that was such a comfort to me. I really needed to talk about, and depend upon the Lord at this time. It was from the Lord that I drew my strength. After talking with Mike, I went back to the hospital to be with Bob for awhile, and then came home to bed. What a long, exhausting day it had been.

Bob recovered so well, he came home on Saturday morning April 6th, 1985. We had a truck load of flowers and well wishes. I felt so supported and loved by family and friends.

EMBRACING DEATH

God alone is my refuge, my place of safety,
He is my God and I am trusting Him.

Psalm 91:2 The Living Bible

CHAPTER 7

A few days later, fear began to creep in once again. I was concerned that as the tumor began to grow on Bob's liver, he would be afraid to die. I opened my Bible and was reading in Ps: 112 from the Living Bible, when verses 6-8 jumped off the page at me. Verse 6: "Such a man will not be overthrown by evil circumstances. God's constant care of him will make a deep impression on all who see it." Verse 7: "He does not fear bad news, nor live in dread of what may happen. For he is settled in his mind that Jehovah will take care of him." Verse 8: "That is why he is not afraid but can calmly face his foes." I could not believe what I was reading. It was just what I needed to hear from God. God was not only taking care of Bob, but He was also taking care of me. I thanked the Lord and was comforted.

Later that week we went to Seattle to see the Oncologist. The news was not good and we were not given much hope. Bob had two choices: he could have heavy- duty chemo, which would give him one chance out of six that he may have a few extra months, or he could choose to do nothing at all and let the cancer run its course, hoping his own immune system would fight it. No matter what choice he made it was a terminal diagnosis. Bob asked how much time he had, and of course the doctor could not say for sure; "maybe one year, maybe two, maybe less." I felt like I had been kicked in the stomach and I could not imagine how Bob was feeling. He was leaning towards taking no treatment.

On our walk back to the car, Bob said "Wow, just five years." I wondered where he came up with five years when the doctor had said one or two years. I then realized his mind could not absorb the devastating and shocking news. I had read somewhere, that sometimes, your brain will shut down when news is too traumatic. The mind goes into shock for awhile; which is a defense mechanism.

As we drove home Bob asked what it would mean for me if he died. How would I handle being alone.? He asked, "Would you stay in Bellingham, or would you move back to British Columbia where your parents and sisters are?" It was so hard to know what to say. I remember a quick, sharp feeling of anger sweeping over me. Why would he ask me that? How could I know, when I was in shock. Sorrow was beginning to overtake me. I wanted to be quiet and let the tears come, but I was too dazed to let that happen. It seemed as though Bob needed to talk, and I did not want to stop him from having that release. It was a hard conversation for both of us.

Bob was showing compassion for me, and that felt good. He talked about how he felt about dying, and where his faith was in the process. He said he had no doubt he was going to be with Jesus, but that when it came right down to the point of knowing you are going to die, you really begin to think through what you believe. He said, "It's easy to say the words, but now comes the time when my trust and faith come into play." My heart ached for him, but I was so proud of him. I could not imagine what it would be like to face your own death.

Even though it was such a difficult conversation for us, it was a time of real closeness. For the first time we were communicating on a deep level. Most of our communication throughout our marriage had been superficial. We usually made jokes and laughed about everything, so we didn't have to face what we were really feeling. We never got past the surface to our deeper feelings. What a shame it took us all these years, and a tragedy like this to happen, before we were able to really talk to each other. How sad that we were so into ourselves, and our own pain, that we could not reach out to each other. We still had not cried together very much; we were still too numb and in shock, but all that was about to change.

The day after our trip to Seattle, I was driving home for lunch from my job when the impact of Bob's cancer and possible death hit me. It was like a dark blackness engulfed me. I felt like a heavy, thick blanket had fallen over me and it was hard to breath. I wanted to let go and weep and wail. I had such a deep sorrow and grieving in my spirit, for both Bob, and myself. I was in so much pain I pulled over to the curb and parked. I cried hard gut - wrenching sobs that felt like they came from the very core of my being. What would life be like without my husband?

I was only eighteen when I met Bob. Our marriage

had been extremely difficult for the first ten years, then I became a Christian and God worked in my life for the next ten years. When Bob also became a Christian and began to change so much, with the Lord's help, after over twenty years we were finally getting it together. Even with all the struggles we had been through, I loved him so much and loved being married. What would it be like being on my own again? I did not even want to think about it. It scared me to death. Who would I call when I needed help? What if the car broke down? What if it was snowy, and the roads were icy? Bob was always there to drive me where I needed to go. Fear began to overtake me.

After I had cried awhile, I felt a release. I picked up my bible that I carried in the car and turned to Psalm 116:1-7 NKJ. I had been reading in the Psalms a lot. Verse 1 begins, "I love the Lord, because he has heard my voice and my supplication. Because He has inclined His ear to me, therefore I will call upon Him as long as I live. The pains of death encompassed me. And the pangs of Sheol laid hold of me. I found trouble and sorrow. Then I called upon the name of the Lord. 'Oh Lord, I implore you. Deliver my soul!' Gracious is the Lord, and righteous; yes our God is merciful. The Lord preserves the simple, I was brought low and he saved me. Return to your rest, O my soul. For the Lord has dealt bountifully with you". And Ps116: 15 NKJ: says "Precious in the sight of the Lord, is the death of His saints'. I found solace in Ps116: 17 NKJ: "I will offer to you the sacrifice of thanksgiving. And will call upon the name of the Lord."

What a comfort to know that Bob's death would be

precious to the Lord. Those scriptures picked me up out of my depression and I could have peace again. I was learning what it meant to give a sacrifice of thanksgiving and praise to the Lord. It is easy to be thankful when things are going well, but not when hard times come along. I knew I needed to be thankful if I was to have peace. What could I be thankful for in the middle of such pain? Certainly, I was not thankful that Bob had cancer, but I could be thankful that we both knew the Lord and He was walking with us. I was thankful that God had given Bob to me as my husband. For the times I had not been thankful for that, I prayed God would forgive me. I would not be who I am today without all the lessons I learned from being married to Bob. I continued to pray; "Forgive me Lord, for trying to run my own marriage for so long and not letting you lead. You have truly taken our brokenness and made something beautiful." Ecclesiastes 3: 1 NKJ says, "He has made everything beautiful in its time." It is in your time Lord, not mine. If you had rescued me from those years of pain, I would have missed so many lessons along the way. It would have stunted my spiritual growth.

I was reminded of the story of the man who felt sorry for the butterfly who was struggling to leave the cocoon. He cut the tissue around the cocoon so the butterfly could get out without struggling, but when it escaped without the struggle it was severely underdeveloped. Its body was small and wrinkled; its wings were crumpled, and it spent its very brief life incapable of flight. Part of the process was to go through the struggle so that it could develop into a strong beautiful butterfly.

I thank you Lord for allowing me to go through all the pain in my life so I could come forth, a maturing Christian. I am sure there is a lot more to come and that is where sacrifice happens. It is hard and sacrificial to praise you during the painful times but I can rejoice knowing you are in it with me, and that I was becoming more capable of loving myself and others, and will come forth more fully developed in my Christian walk and relationship with you.

CHAPTER 8

In the weeks that followed we talked a lot about death and dying. Bob said, "It is so hard to prepare for you own death." We read everything we could in the Bible about heaven. A friend suggested we read a book called 'Within Heavens Gates' by Rebecca Springer. The author shares her personal vision and experience of a visit to Heaven. That little book encouraged us so much. The author's account of Heaven was so beautiful. I said to Bob, "How come you get to go and I have to stay behind?"

Another book we read was 'Facing Death', by Billy Graham. It was extremely practical and helpful. It taught Bob how to get his affairs in order. In his book, Dr. Graham talked about how we plan for our wedding, but never our funeral. After reading that book Bob decided we should go to the funeral home and take care of our arrangements. Neither one of these books were the least bit depressing to us but instead, were deeply encouraging. We both felt that this encouragement had to be from God. We were facing reality, and God was blessing us for it. Sometimes, when I would cry and grieve over his dying, Bob would look at me and say, "You know, only God knows when the time is for either one of us to die. You could be crossing the street and be hit by a truck and go first, for all we know." Oh what a scary thought!! I knew that was true and look at all the energy I would have spent feeling sorry for both of us, wasting the precious time we had left. Often we encouraged each other with those words, and strangely enough, they were comforting.

Bob had decided he wanted to be cremated and have his ashes scattered. One of his friends asked him to think about how his children might view this decision. On the advice of his friend, we decided to talk to our children. They all agreed we should have a plot with a marker so they would be able to come and visit at the cemetery and bring our grandchildren even though we did not yet have any grandchildren. Again, there were a lot of tears making these decisions, but we also felt the Lord's comfort with us. Bob was so courageous during this talk, it strengthened all of us. He told the kids we would buy a plot, but that there was another option he might choose. He said that he could have half his ashes buried and the other half scattered. He would not tell them which half was in the ground so they would not know which end of him they were talking to, we all laughed so that broke the tension. We were thankful he still had his wonderful sense of humor.

Bob told me he did not want his mother and I coming out and sitting in the car by the graveside every day crying and mourning. He was sure she would want to do that, and he was trying to protect me from further pain. He and I both knew he would be with the Lord and not at the cemetery. Sometimes when we talked about Heaven, Bob would say, "I feel sorry for you because you are going to have to stay here and try to comfort my mother." Their relationship had been difficult over the years and he knew she would have a hard time accepting his death. One day when Bob came home for lunch, he asked, "Do you think you will remarry ?." I did not know how to answer him. Of course I had thought about it because I really liked being married. I was sure if I said yes it would hurt him, and if I said no, that I would not remarry, that might hurt him as well. I was concerned he might think, was our marriage so bad she would not do it again? I thought for a minute as I threw up my arrow prayer, "Lord help; What do I say." I finally gave Bob my answer; "You know I want to serve the Lord the rest of my life and it would be up to Him. It would be easier to serve the Lord as a single person, but whatever God's plan is for me, I will be open to it." Whew!! I sent another arrow prayer. "Thank you Lord for giving me that bit of wisdom so I didn't have to hurt him." Bob seemed satisfied. He said, "I hope you do meet someone. You deserve a good Christian husband." I felt that was sweet of him to say. I said I would like to take some training and maybe go into counseling, something I had been interested in since I was a young girl and certainly had experience with this subject. It was a hard conversation, but when we talked like this, I felt such deep love and closeness to him.

CHAPTER 9

Almost two years had gone by since the first diagnosis. Bob had already outlived the doctors predicted timeline. Though he was feeling pretty well physically, he was often quite depressed. I tried to give him his space and let him experience his feelings during the down times. I sensed he needed to process this on his own but sometimes the pain would overwhelm me as I watched him go through these heart wrenching times Since we had never been through anything like this, we didn't know what to expect. Would he gradually deteriorate or would our worst fear materialize, where one day he would just suddenly drop dead.

In February, 1987, Bob's blood count went from 7.5 to 44, which meant the tumor was growing. He was still enjoying golfing with his friends on Wednesdays, and on Saturdays we would visit Vancouver B.C., and walk around the seawall at Stanley Park. The path was built along the Oceanside, and we sometimes walked seven miles from the entrance on Georgia Street, around the inner harbour, under the Lions Gate bridge, past prospect point to English

Bay and then onwards to the Sylvia hotel. There are three different beaches along the way, and we often stopped and had our lunch while we rested. We would see numerous freighters in the harbour, waiting to come in, and unload their merchandise before they would load up again. Cruise ships would pass by, and small power boats and sailboats would be coming and going. At times we would walk along the beautiful, meandering paths through the park. We would pass the quiet still waters of Lost Lagoon, and stroll through the Rose Garden. Sometimes we would walk through the zoo, and stop to see the monkeys, penguins and other exotic animals.

Because of the gorgeous ocean views, we enjoyed walking around the outside perimeter the most. We would sit for a time on a bench overlooking the ocean, watching a Seaplane taking off, or a tugboat coming in with a barge, listening to the waves lapping up against the rocks on the shore. It was such a peaceful time for us. Bob would have his arm around me or hold my hand as we walked. I felt like I was in heaven myself, it meant so much to me to have him show affection.

Bob began to open up and share his feelings. He talked about how he felt about the Lord and said I was the one he wanted to talk to about spiritual things. Wow! That was so new to me and I loved it. He said, "All my adult life when I had a problem, I would not talk about it but instead turn to alcohol to numb the pain. Now I can no longer drink because I know it would be too hard on my liver, so I have to face my thoughts, and the idea of my dying without alcohol." My heart went out to him, it must have been terribly hard for him. We had fought many times over the years about his drinking and I had begged him to quit. After the diagnosis, he said; "And I suppose you want me to give up alcohol." I did not feel it was my place to tell him what to do so I said," Bob, it is your decision, you know how hard alcohol is on your liver, and it will already be fighting the cancer, but it is up to you. It is your life and your decision." He decided to quit drinking. I was so relieved and thankful.

Bob was drawn to Stanley Park, and said he felt so comforted with me beside him. I would quietly pray, "Lord, thank you for the love you have given us for each other." We began going every weekend on Saturday, then coming again on Sunday. Our friends, Art and Evelyn would sometimes meet us and walk around the park with us. They had a suite in their home and invited us to come and stay over on Saturday nights so we would not have to drive so far the next day. They called it 'The McQuarrie Suite.' We were so grateful to them, and to God, for His goodness to us.

In the nice weather we would lie on the grass overlooking English Bay and be warmed by the sun. We walked in the rain, wind, or whatever the weather conditions presented. It was such a healing time for us and our love for God and each other grew deeper. Bob seemed to be drawing closer to the Lord as well. It was about this time he wrote this letter yielding himself to God.

Feb. 9/85

This day I am giving all my problems over to the Lord, trusting in him that he will take over my life and guide me in the right direction, with peace of mind.

R.B. McQuarrie

Sometimes it was hard for us to believe Bob was really sick because he looked so healthy and partly because we wanted him to be well. We were finally enjoying a love and closeness we had not experienced before and neither one of us wanted it to end.

CHAPTER 10

In September, 1987, the blood tests went from 44 to 190, showing considerable tumor activity. The Cat Scan showed more spots on the liver, Bob seemed to handle the news well. I had a sinking feeling in my stomach, and I could physically feel my heart ache. Fear was beginning to overtake me, was this the beginning of the end?

Clay called that evening, and as Bob shared the test results with him, they cried together. Jennie called in the morning and as I shared the outcome of the tests with her, we too cried together. Now we had to let Mike and Patti know about the results of the tests. The next week we went to see the oncologist in Seattle again. He wanted Bob to take Chemo right away. He asked Bob to try it for three months If there was no improvement, Bob would be hospitalized for four days and they would shoot the chemotherapy continually into the liver. He would be very sick and loose his hair with the last alternative. Once again, Bob struggled with what to do.

Bob chose not to take any treatment and hard as it was, I supported him in this decision. At best, the treatment would extend his life for a few months but he did not think it was worth it. A few more months of misery did not appeal to Bob, especially when he was feeling good right now and having a hard time believing he even had cancer. I had been reading a lot about vitamins and minerals; how a lot of our foods were depleted of nutrients because of the sprays and chemicals we were using. I was taking extra vitamins myself so we decided to go to the health food store and talk with them. We knew it would not cure Bob, however we wanted to do everything we could to give him the best quality of life during the time he had left.

We were advised about liver cleanses and given a variety of natural vitamins. Our family doctor was concerned that I was thinking this would be a cure, but after we talked awhile he understood, and accepted, our decision. As time went on the doctor was pleased with how well Bob was doing and whenever we went for an appointment he would ask "Are you still taking your vitamins?" While this may not be for everyone, the vitamins and minerals seemed to be working for us, at least making us feel we were doing all we could to keep Bob strong.

CHAPTER 11

In October, 1987, we had planned a weekend with the children in Vancouver, at the Sylvia hotel. Before we left, we called them together and showed them the X-rays. We talked about Bob's decision and why he made it; he said for the time he had left, he wanted it to be quality time rather than a mere quantity of time. We had a lot of tears but the kids were supportive of Bob's decision not to seek treatment. Somehow, we managed to put the reality of what was happening behind us and had a wonderful time together, in spite of knowing the cancer was progressing rapidly.

When we arrived for our weekend in Vancouver, Bob and the kids rented bikes and rode around the seawall at Stanley Park. Since I had never learned to ride a bike I joined them at the end of their journey. We then played Pitch and Putt golf together before going to dinner. The next morning we had a lovely brunch, then the guys went to play golf, while the girls and I did some shopping.

We were beginning to feel Stanley Park was our haven of rest. When we were in the park, we felt so close to God and each other. It meant so much to Bob to have his family around him and to let them share our special place.

In November, 1987, Bob was feeling pretty well, so we decided to take a trip to Florida. Since we had never been to Florida, it seemed like a good idea at the time. We flew to Orlando and rented a car. We visited Disney World, Cape Canaveral, and drove down to Clearwater for a few days. Bob was in a quiet, reflective mood most of the week and I felt shut out again. That hurt so much, but I guessed it was part of the dying process for him. After we got home he told me he had a hard time on trips now. He said all he wanted to do is spend more time with the kids and not take any more trips without them, as it made him feel too far away from them.

He decided to plan a trip to Hawaii, in March 1988, and pay the airfare so that all the children could come with us. They managed to get the time off work, and stayed with us for the first week, we had the second week by ourselves. We rented a condo on the beach at Maui, and every evening we sat on the deck enjoying watching the whales frolicking and spouting water as they moved from one area to another. Bob felt pretty good when the kids were there, but the second week, he was having a lot of stomach distress and wasn't eating well. He was exhausted. We thought maybe he had overdone it the week before, and we were glad to get home. I realized this would probably be our last long trip anywhere.

In January 1988, Bob had more blood tests done and the results were not good. Since returning from our Florida trip he had been having severe pain in his right side. The doctor said he could now feel the tumors on his liver. Bob asked the doctor if he thought he would have another year and the doctor said he thought it would be less than a year. We both struggled with that painful news. We knew we would hear this news eventually, however we were not ready yet and it was heartbreaking to hear.

Would Bob be here for the upcoming holidays this year: Valentine's Day, Easter, July 4th, Thanksgiving, or Christmas? I struggled with the thought of him not being with us. We cried and hugged each other, as we anticipated what every ache and pain meant. It was agonizing when Bob got the flu and was sick for four days, we didn't know what was happening. We were relieved later, when I also got sick because we then knew it was just the flu and Bob was not dying, yet.

One Sunday morning, I was feeling very weepy so instead of going to church, I drove to the beautiful Boulevard Park, which looks over Bellingham Bay. I parked the car and watched the wind playing with the ocean, churning up the waves, and throwing them against the rocks. I felt the tears coming and I rolled up the windows so I could let go completely and have a good cry; actually it was more like a good wail. I felt the weight of everything come crushing down on me as the sobs came from the very depth of my being, wracking my whole body. I felt completely alone, realizing I was carrying everyone else's pain. I knew the children's pain was not mine to carry. I now know it would have helped if I could have talked to them about their feelings, but I just could not at the time. I recognized my children were suffering, but we never talked about how they felt. Looking back, I wished we were more able to talk about our feelings with each other. I loved Bob and my children so dearly, it was painful watching them suffer.

I cried until I felt like there were no more tears left in me. I took my Bible and turned to the Psalms: Ps 34:18 NIV, jumped out at me, "The Lord is close to the brokenhearted and saves those who are crushed in spirit." That was exactly how I felt, completely crushed. Then I read Ps 38: 21 and 22 NIV. "Lord do not forsake me, do not be far from me, O my God. Come quickly to help me O Lord my Savior." I felt the Lord's goodness towards me. Those scriptures were exactly what I needed. I continued to pray for Bob's healing, but felt in my spirit this would not be the outcome.

Bob had not been feeling well since our trip to Hawaii. He was having stomach cramps and headaches, as well as feeling pain above his left ear, and down the side of his head. The headaches lasted a few days, and then would go away only to return once again. The medication for his stomach was making him very tired and was not helping so it was discontinued. He had another Cat Scan and the results were not good: the cancer now covered over sixty percent of his liver. Our doctor said he could not believe Bob's stamina and how well he was functioning with so much of his liver affected. Both our family doctor and our oncologist, were hesitant to give a time frame, however, both felt that Bob didn't have more than six months to live, probably closer to three months. In our spirits, Bob and I felt it would be soon, but to hear this news from the doctors hit us like a ton of bricks. Once again the numbness overtook us.

CHAPTER 12

In the spring of 1988, Bob planned a fishing trip into the interior of British Columbia, with his step- brother John and our sons, Clay and Mike. He said he wanted some one- on- one time with his sons, which they had, but unfortunately he spent most of the weekend sick in bed, and due to his illness, it was a disappointment to all of them.

Bob decided to quit work at the end of July, 1988. Jennie immediately planned a retirement party for him on July 30th. It was a wonderful time, as our children and many of our friends came to encourage and support us. The party was held at Jennie's home. Everyone brought a variety of food and drinks for us to enjoy.

It was around this time that Bob began to look into our financial status, and our medical policies. We would only have medical coverage for eighteen months after he quit work. We knew it would be expensive, and wondered if we could afford to pay for all our expenses, having no income? I knew it was a hard decision for Bob to make.

I never heard Bob complain or feel sorry for himself. His bravery was a great gift to all of us. In a time of such deep sorrow, Bob continued to be an example of strength and dignity to his family. Because of the way he handled his condition, we, as a family, could draw from his strength. One day he asked me if I felt cheated, I asked, "Do you?" He never really answered so maybe he was wondering why his life was being cut short? He was only fifty-four and I was forty- eight, some of the best years of our lives should have been ahead of us. We agreed the Lord was walking with us, comforting us with his presence, but we still needed to grieve and experience all the emotions that go along with the process of dying.

The weight of the terminal cancer was heavy upon me. Not knowing from one day to the next what was going to happen, was almost unbearable. So often, I could feel myself giving in to fear and concern for my future. What will happen to me? How will I make it on my own? Would I stay in Bellingham or move back to Canada? I began to realize I would soon be walking alone. I prayed again, "Oh God help me. I am sinking again. Oh Lord, I am going to become a widow, just as you had said to me long ago".

The separation had begun. I felt Bob pulling away from me again, retreating into himself. He had always been one to keep to himself and found it hard to let others come close, but lately, he had been opening up to me so I felt the pain more deeply whenever he would withdraw again. The nurse shared with me that when a person is dying, they often pull away as they are trying to say goodbye to this life, and getting ready for the next. Therefore, I tried to be understanding.

Bob had another appointment with the oncologist in

Seattle and announced that it did not matter to him if I joined him or not. He would just as soon go by himself. Those words cut through my heart like a knife! After that conversation, when I was by myself, I cried and cried, fighting back the anger that was welling up inside me. I thought to myself, "I am your wife. Why won't you let me share your life, your pain, and your sorrows? I felt so alone, a feeling I had experienced many times in our marriage. The old familiar feelings of anger and resentment that were hidden deep inside me were rearing their ugly heads. Then I remembered what the nurse said about dying people withdrawing. I decided to respect Bob's need to withdraw and give him his space, no matter how much it hurt me. I began to pray, "Lord, I am thankful for the times Bob has let me into his life."

CHAPTER 13

Bob had expressed in the past that he would like to try his hand at painting. He had shown an artistic talent over the years, so as a gift for our anniversary on August 14th, I bought him a series of painting lessons, with oils. I thought it would help take his mind off the cancer and help him to relax. He did beautiful work and enjoyed the classes immensely.

I think we were all surprised at Bob's amazing talent. He left us with many treasured paintings, and he even sold a few of them. He made sure each one of the children chose a special painting for themselves. Most of his paintings were of scenery but he painted some pictures of flowers in vases as well. I was amazed at the beauty of the flowers; they were soft and gentle with drops of dew on the petals. I saw the gentleness of his spirit come out in his paintings. He expressed how sorry he was that he had not started painting years ago.

During August and September, Bob was fighting depression. He said he wanted to die at home so the doctor said it was time to call Hospice. When we met with Hospice, it was decided that they would provide a nurse once a week, until further care was needed.

In early August, Bob was put on morphine to ease the pain in his stomach and side. He was having cramps that were painful at times. The morphine took care of the pain, however it was hard to regulate. Too much morphine made him sleepy so he could not function, and not enough morphine, did nothing to control the pain. Bob had not been feeling well since he quit work at the end of July. He was hoping to take some short trips to the Oregon Coast, and Vancouver Island, but he was not feeling well enough to even go to Stanley Park, for a day trip.

We had planned a trip with our friends, Jim and Shar Bath to celebrate our anniversary. They took their fifty-two foot yacht up to Pender Harbour and we were supposed to drive up and meet them there so that we could spend a few days on the boat. They had been so good to us, inviting us often to spend time with them, and it was one of our favorite things to do. Bob had been depressed and not feeling well the week before, so I wondered if we should go. I called the doctor and he said if Bob felt physically up to going, the trip might be good for him. Bob insisted, so we decided to go.

Sunday was our anniversary. We had not been getting gifts for each other for several years, as we usually went somewhere for the weekend instead, so it was a surprise to me that when we got up in the morning in the hotel, Bob presented me with the most beautiful diamond ring I had ever seen. What a lovely surprise; I had no idea he was going to give me a gift. We both cried and held each other tight, knowing this would be our last anniversary.

We met the Bath's the next day and had a wonderful two days cruising around the harbour. On the drive home, Bob had planned another surprise. We pulled off the highway at Secret Cove, and I discovered he had made reservations for a little cabin on the beach. We could hear the waves lapping up against the rocks outside our door as we looked out over the ocean, observing the uninhabited islands in front of our cabin. What a bittersweet time. I prayed "Lord, I can't believe with all the pain and depression he has been going through, he would think to plan all this for me and make it so special. It is truly a miracle how far you have brought us since the early days in our marriage." No wonder Bob insisted that we come after all the work he had gone to making these plans. I loved Bob so much it was painful. My heart was breaking when I thought our marriage would soon be over, but it was comforting to know we both believed we would be together for all eternity.

Labor Day weekend, Bob stayed in bed most of the weekend. By this time I was also feeling depressed. I felt overwhelmed, like I was on an emotional rollercoaster. The entire weekend I felt like I was getting a glimpse of what it would be like after he was gone. The loneliness was weighing on me like a thick blanket. Because he was in bed so much lately, we kept thinking he was going to die any minute. His blood pressure was low the last time the nurse took it, and that scared me. I called the hospice nurse and she came over to see him. She said he was a long way from dying, because his heart was so strong. Since his stomach had been bothering him, the doctor prescribed some ulcer medication and Bob began to feel much better.

Our former Young Life Area Director, Jim Eney, came to see Bob. Bob had always loved Jim and asked him if he would give the eulogy at his funeral. I left them alone for awhile, grateful for the opportunity to have a break. Bob said they had a good visit, even though he cried through most of it. I loved it when Jim came to visit; he was not afraid to ask direct questions about how Bob spent his time: if he was talking with the Lord and thinking about heaven, or if he was at peace about leaving his family, with the assurance that he will be with Jesus? I realized if I had asked similar things it would have seemed like I was nagging. I was grateful to Jim for asking the hard questions.

So many friends and family stopped by to visit. All the children were so thoughtful to come and stay overnight with me, as I needed them. I will never be able to express to them my gratitude for how they lovingly cared for Bob and I.

September had been a hard month. Physically Bob was feeling better, however because of his depression, he decided to take to his bed and was on the verge of giving up. Our family came together and decided we needed to help him get out of bed and take part in life once again. We tried to take him out to the park, for a drive in the car, or to see a movie, anything to help him get his mind on other things. But Bob would not hear of it. He said he was just waiting to die and wished the Lord would take him. It was hard to watch him hurting, and yet he was unable to do anything to help himself.

Thursday September 29th, is a day I will never forget. Once again Bob lay in bed most of the morning. He did not seem to be in physical pain, but he was severely depressed, almost belligerent and very unpleasant to be around, this had been going on for days. I sat on the bed and tried to talk with him. He was angry and once again said he wanted to die, and asked why the Lord would not take him. It seemed as though he wanted me to give him the answers that only the Lord could give him.

All of a sudden, it felt like I had all I could take! The pressure of this emotional rollercoaster had been building up like a volcano inside me and the lid was about to pop off, and I was helpless to stop it. I had tried to be strong, as I did not want to make it any harder for Bob. I knew he was getting closer to the Lord, and was reading his Bible a lot, but that was something he only wanted to share with me, most of his friends did not even know he was a Christian.

I felt like Bob was drawing from my faith and sucking all the strength out of me. I could not bear the weight of feeling responsible for his spiritual comfort and growth. Bob continued asking me why God would not take him. I did not know either, and had some of the same questions. I could hardly bear the pain. I said, "Bob the Lord has been trying to reach you for years and you would never give in to Him. You said yourself, whenever you had a problem you would turn to drink to escape, but from this problem you can't run away. Now, you want the Lord to take you as your way of escape."

I could feel anger welling up in me. "You are still trying to run things your way and be in control. The Lord will take you when He is ready and not before. Do you plan to spend the next month or two, or however long you have, laying in bed and being miserable with everyone around you and angry at God because you do not have control? Try to count your blessings, among them being the four wonderful children we have and concentrate on the good things about your life and enjoy the rest of it the best you can." Then I walked out of the room crying. Once in the living room I began to pray, "Oh God forgive me if I was too harsh with him. I can't even imagine what he must be going through. I can never fully appreciate how Bob feels. It must be so hard for him. He keeps reaching out to me for answers to help him through. It kills me to think I may have added to his hurt. Lord, forgive me."

Later in the afternoon Bob got up, came out in the living

room and I could feel something had changed in him. He had a different air about him. He suggested we go for a ride to Bulevard Park. It was so good walking together along the path on the water's edge. It is such a beautiful park, and we both loved the ocean. We never talked about it again, but that conversation (one sided as it was) seemed to be a turning point for Bob and I, his whole attitude had changed.

The next Saturday, Bob said he wanted to go to Stanley Park. I called Clay and asked if he would drive. When the day came Bob decided he would drive. We had a nice lunch in Vancouver and a good visit with Clay. Bob drove us home again. It was like a miracle because he had not driven or been out of the house for two weeks. Later, he confided in me that he was testing himself, because he wanted us to take a trip across the North Cascades highway. Once again I prayed, "Thank you Lord for the change in him."

On Thursday October 6th, we were able to fulfill Bob's desire to take the North Cascades Highway trip. Jennie accompanied us in case Bob needed her to help with the driving. We drove over the North Cascades, and back through Stevens Pass. The fall colors were beautiful, with the leaves on the trees, shining gloriously, in bright yellow, orange and red colors. It was wonderful to be with our daughter Jennie. It was hard for both of us to see Bob deteriorating, we shed some tears when she and I got a few moments alone. Bob and I agreed, this could possibly be our last trip together.

During the rest of October, friends came to visit, and this was a real comfort and blessing to both of us. Bob was in pain so I talked to the nurse about increasing the morphine, and that seemed to help.

Bob and I had a good talk about how this was affecting our children. I could see that God softened Bob's heart as he shared that he wanted to talk with each of his children separately. He shared that he wanted them to forgive him for anything he may have done or neglected to do, and he was concerned they may be holding anger. I prayed, "Lord help him to have the courage and give him the right words to say when he talks to the children". I was so proud of Bob for doing this. He said he knew that he had been extra hard on Clay, and Jennie, while they were growing up and he needed to know they forgave him. Bob was sorry he had not spent more time with his children and he wanted this included in his eulogy.

CHAPTER 14

One day out of the blue, Bob said, "We probably won't be going out much anymore so I think you should get yourself a cat." I thought, 'What, are you kidding me'? I couldn't believe it, Bob had never liked cats, especially in the house, and as we lived in a condo this would definitely have to be an inside cat. I knew he was doing this for me, and it touched me deeply.

After looking in the paper, I found a beautiful little black and white kitten. Bob named the cat 'Boots' because he had four white paws. It was fun to watch as Bob and Boots played together. Boots ended up giving Bob a lot of enjoyment.

By the middle of October, the morphine was once again increased, relieving more of the pain. Bob had been throwing up, but that had finally stopped as well. I thanked the Lord, as that had been hard to watch. Now Bob was losing a lot of weight and his color was not good, but I was thankful he was not in as much pain, and he was much more loving. He seemed to be through the anger stage.

Bob's anger of dealing with cancer and his prognosis had been so hard on both of us.

As the Lord drew Bob and I into a deeper relationship with each other, we sensed it was now time to prepare for final arrangements. Our first decision was to go to Bayview cemetery to pick out a burial plot. We agreed quickly, and were pleased with our choice of a plot on a hillside under a maple tree. The next day we went to the funeral home and picked out a headstone; one day my ashes would be buried with Bob's, so we needed a headstone that would be for both of us. I was soon to discover that this day would be quite different from the day before - it reflected the difficulty we had experienced previously in our relationship.

Over the years we had such a hard time agreeing on so many things and now we could not even agree on a headstone. Eventually both our names would be on it, causing each of us to have strong opinions on what we wanted. He wanted brown and I wanted grey. The plaque would read Robert B. McQuarrie on one side and Patricia R. McQuarrie on the other. He wanted 'Bob' in brackets, I did not want 'Pat' in brackets. I wanted scripture and praying hands, and he wanted Fir trees.

It struck us both as comical, that we were struggling over how our headstone would read, and finally both of us gave a little until we came to an agreement. As we struggled, it showed me how strong we could both be when something is important to us. The scripture and praying hands were important to me, so they stayed. Bob had Fir trees by his name, and we put the praying hands close to where my name would eventually be. The scripture from

2 Corinthians 5:8 that says something similar to; "To be absent from the body is to be present with the Lord", was placed across the bottom. We had a good laugh on the way home about what a struggle it had been to make the final arrangements, however, we were both happy with the end results.

A few days later, the funeral home called to say that the headstone was ready to view. Even though Bob was not doing well, I knew he wanted to see it, so we decided to go together. The headstone was lovely, and we were pleased because it was just how we wanted it to look.

We thought this whole process would be depressing, but instead the Lord had given us peace.

CHAPTER 15

In November, as we were lying in bed, I noticed that Bob's breathing pattern was changing. He was taking short breaths, with long pauses in between. At times they were very loud, and at other times, very quiet. It was scary because his breathing was so irregular. Sometimes I could count to five between breaths, and sometimes all the way to ten or twelve. I would ask myself, is this the end? I never knew.

I knew that a change in breathing was one of the signs the end was near. Bob was spending more time in bed now. He began to express there were times he was scared and felt his death would be soon. He was having trouble keeping food down. The tumors in his stomach felt hard and continued to grow. With every new episode of vomiting, breathing difficulties, and his long hours of sleep, fear was beginning to overtake us.

In order to keep my stress down, I continued swimming at the community pool even though for some time now, I was not comfortable leaving Bob alone. The children and I felt it was important for me to continue exercising and they were so good to come and stay with him, allowing me to take some much needed time for myself. Mike was especially helpful, as he was the one living closest to us. Patti came midweek for a couple of days, and Clay, Jennie and Mike would alternate on the weekends. It was comforting having them around, they were such a help to both of us. Our friends were so supportive and came often to see him, however, because Bob was getting too exhausted, we were now at the point where we had to limit visitors.

Twice in one week, I dreamed that Bob passed away. I had a physical pain in my chest and woke up wimpering, feeling the full force of crushing sorrow. It was actually physically painful; I was shocked at how much it hurt. I turned to the Lord once again and prayed, "Oh Lord, I suppose it is a glimpse of the loneliness ahead for me. I will not dwell on the loneliness, because you say in your Word you will never leave me or forsake me. You have been with me this far, and at times I have felt your presence so strongly. I love you Lord for walking closely with me through this horrendously painful time, as I walk through the valley of the shadow of my husband's death."

The next time the hospice nurse came she felt it was time to order a hospital bed. After she left, Bob and I held each other and cried. We were at a new stage in the progression of his illness and it was heart - wrenching for us. As difficult as the transition of seeing Bob in a hospital bed was for me, I knew it would be hard on Bob and our children as well.

On the morning of Nov 9th, 1988, I arranged for the bed to be delivered while Bob was sleeping. I wanted it to be ready for him when he woke up, hoping it would be easier on him. I called the children to prepare them before their next visit. I knew it would be difficult to see him in that bed if they were not forewarned. We cried together, and I was so glad that I had shared the news that his hospital bed would be in the living room. I wanted to protect them as much as possible from the shock of seeing their dad's decline.

Actually, the bed worked much better than we had anticipated. When company came and Bob felt tired, he could just doze off, and not feel left out. At the end of the week, all the kids came and in spite of everything, we had a good time. I thanked the Lord for being so good and giving us a wonderful weekend together.

By mid November Bob spent most of his time in bed, but occasionally, he was able to get up and sit on the couch. The hospice nurse informed us he now had a buildup of fluid in his body. She thought he could go at anytime because he was so peaceful. Bob had become very quiet. He could not talk about how he felt, and was withdrawing into himself. He seemed so distant. Now he was throwing up even when he brushed his teeth. I would go in and rub his back when he was wretching. I could feel how thin he had become and was grieved as I felt his boney shoulders, and his body wasting away. I admired his courage as he went through this. I never heard him complain. He still had his wonderful sense of humor and would make a joke of some kind, causing us both to laugh. How I loved him and wished his suffering would end soon. I was so thankful that because of medication he was not in a lot of pain.

All of our children, and Bob's mom were with us for Thanksgiving. It was difficult as we knew it would be our last Thanksgiving together. We had a lovely traditional turkey dinner with all the trimmings, and later we played a family game of Trivial Pursuit while Bob rested.

The Sunday after Thanksgiving, Bob woke up feeling very restless. He said he could not lie down, could not stand, or sit up. He was not able to explain what he was feeling. He expressed to me that he just could not be still. He had been depressed since Thanksgiving, but he was now more and more anxious. He spent a lot of time pacing. I wondered if his restlessness was because he was thinking about how I would manage after he was gone.

At the end of November, Bob and I sat down together so he could show me the budget and what needed to be paid each month. Since the beginning of our marriage, Bob had always taken care of the bills. He always gave me an allowance to take care of groceries and anything the children would need. He expressed he did not want me writing checks even though we had a joint account, because he said my handwriting was like chicken scratch (which was true), and he did not want to mess up the look of the check register. How's that for a perfectionist? I have to say he had beautiful handwriting. Because Bob was such a detail-oriented person, his handling of our finances worked well for us, so it was hard for him to turn this responsibility over to me. Bookwork was a favorite thing for Bob and he always enjoyed doing the bills, however, as his health declined he would get mixed up and as he could no longer write legibly, he was not able to keep the register accurate.

The differences in my husband were more pronounced now. Bob shuffled when he walked, his voice was very weak, and most of the time he could not keep food down. He had lost so much weight and kept looking at himself in the mirror, probably hoping what he saw was not a true reflection of him. I would tell Bob he was still the most handsome man I knew, but I do not think he believed me.

It was difficult to plan for Christmas. I prayed and asked the Lord, "Will Bob even be here? I think we should go ahead and plan as usual, and if he isn't here, what better place for him to be than with you Lord? What a joyful Christmas that would be for him. Lord,help me; I need to keep that thought in mind as I go through this holiday season." Again the thought came to me 'to be absent from the body is to be present with the Lord.' I thanked the Lord for reminding me, as it was so comforting to me.

On December 1ˢᵗ, I went out and bought a Christmas tree. That had always been so much fun for Bob and I to do together. There were times when we would go as a family up to Mt. Baker and bring home a tree. Bob loved hauling it home and decorating it with the children. I pretended to help, but truthfully, I never enjoyed decorating the tree much. Bob thanked me for putting the tree up and we had a good cry. At that moment, I realized I would need to get used to decorating the tree by myself now.

Bob thanked me for looking after him through his illness and said how much he appreciated me being there for him. That made me feel so good. He said, "I am sorry for all the rotten things I have ever done to you." While I appreciated him saying it, as I had waited years to hear those words, I needed to hear more. Some specifics, like, what exactly was he sorry for?

When he said he was sorry, immediately pictures came to my mind of all the years of him being out all night, and his womanizing . I needed to talk about these concerns with him now but I was afraid to mention specifics, because I knew if he denied them, as he had done in the past, I would only hurt more and hate him for it. He was dying, and I did not want to hate him. I loved him and I did not want to hurt him. As we were both hurting enough I decided to bury my feelings and deal with them after he was gone, not knowing at the time how hard that would be. So instead, I said, "Thank you. I forgive you." I had forgiven him previously, said the words anyway, but because nothing was ever talked about and resolved, I still felt the pain. This was another sorrow I just could not face right now. I prayed, "Oh Lord, this is so hard and painful. When is it going to end for all of us? I don't know how much more I can take."

CHAPTER 16

The first couple of weeks in December, Bob continued to feel restless. He was pacing, and he could not seem to get settled. He walked around like a zombie, and half the time, he did not respond when I talked to him. He followed me wherever I went, even into the bathroom. He had become like a little child, not letting me out of his sight. He became so thin and looked so haggard now, I hoped he was unaware of how much he had changed. He said he was becoming weaker and more tired, and hoped he could just go to sleep and not wake up; but he told me that this thought also scared him. I encouraged him to think about the Lord and what it will be like to be with Him, rather than dwelling on the fact he was leaving his family behind. I assured him we would be okay, and that the Lord would take care of us.

Each time Bob asked me how much longer it would be, I replied, "Only the Lord knows, Hon." hoping it would be soon for his sake. The last two weeks had been the hardest. I began to pray, "Thank you Lord that Bob knows you and will be with you. Help me be strong and encourage him,

I keep trying to encourage him to read the word, listen to Christian music, and talk to you. I know that would bring comfort to him; at least it does for me. Maybe I am being too pushy with him? Sometimes I don't know what else to do, I want so badly for him to feel your presence. Maybe I should back off and let you do whatever you need to do for him? Forgive me Lord, for thinking I know what he needs. I realize what I am feeling is that if he could turn to you, it would ease my pain. Sometimes I feel he is drawing so much from me that I am drained to the point where I have nothing left to give. How I wish he would draw from you Lord."

The next time the nurse came, Bob told her he felt scared at night when he woke up - not of being dead, but about how he would die. She assured him that as death approached, he would probably become more sleepy might slip into a coma. That seemed to comfort him. I told him I would sleep in the living room, if it would make him feel better. So with the children's help I put a mattress on the floor by Bob's bed and I slept there. As he was becoming more and more restless, we spent most of the night drinking tea together. We talked to the doctor and he adjusted Bob's medication. Thankfully, that helped Bob sleep better.

Our Children took turns coming and staying the night. As the end drew near, Patti came on Sunday and stayed till Wednesday. Jennie came from Wednesday through Friday, and Clay and Mike came on the Weekend. It was such a relief for me to have my children there, as I returned to my own bed and could have uninterrupted sleep. I was able to cope much better when I was rested. What a blessing our children were to us. But, I knew this was terribly hard on them as well.

When the hospice nurse came for her next visit, after taking Bob's vital signs, she said she did not know what was keeping him here. His body seemed ready to go, so she wondered if there could be some reason he was hanging on? Bob continued to ask me for answers that I could not give him, I did not know what to say, so I asked him if he had ever given his body to the Lord? I was thinking of Romans 12:1 NIV: "Therefore, I urge you brothers, in view of God's mercy, to offer your bodies as a living sacrifice, holy and pleasing to God. This is your spiritual act of worship." At the time, Bob was sitting propped up in bed. He said "no", and immediately looked up at the ceiling and said "Lord I give you my body." I was surprised, that this man, who had been resisting my attempts to share scripture with him for so long, was now so eager to receive the comfort of God's word. Looking back, I can see that the acceptance of your own death can be a personal act of worship as you surrender yourself to God.

I had been playing Christmas Carols, and praise and worship music for Bob, while he was resting the last few days. I hoped that would sooth him. One evening while Jennie and I were visiting, we looked over at Bob, to see him sitting up in bed, with his eyes closed, and a smile on his face. He looked so peaceful. What a difference from the painful, troubled look he had lately.

The next morning he came into the bedroom at six am. He seemed excited, and with a big smile said, "the Lord really loves me." I asked what he meant and he said,

"Because I had a good night's sleep last night." It was a comfort to see the transformation in him. He had finally received the peace the Lord had been trying to give him.

As I look back I recognize that dying, unless it is sudden, is a process- our private journey with God, one that only He can accomplish. We cannot bring a person to the place of Godly surrender. This takes an act of God. Dying is a person's most intimate journey between themselves and their God. I was so glad we were able to talk openly about Bob's impending death, which made it easier for all the family to face.

Over Christmas the children stayed with us. The condo was small, but cozy, and we were sleeping all over the place. We were crowded but it felt good to be together. Bob shared with Clay that he had a dream, and the Lord told him he would not die before Christmas. He said he knew it was true because he felt so peaceful. When I found out what Bob had shared with Clay I was so happy for him. I was reminded of a time when Bob was reading his Bible, as he now did daily, and he called me over to see what the Lord had been saying to him through the scriptures. I prayed, "Lord you are so good! Thank you for speaking to Bob's heart."

The next few days were a wonderful time for Bob. I said, "Bob, when you see Jesus, you have to come back and tell us that you saw him before you go." With a smile, he agreed, and promised he would. Christmas Eve, we had our dinner early then Clay, Rae (Bob's mom) and I went to candlelight church service at 11pm.

Christmas morning Bob was up at 6:30am and woke the kids up. He said, "When you were little you got us up at the crack of dawn on Christmas morning. Now it's my turn." He sat with us halfway through our gift opening, and then went back to his bed. As his strength was gone, I opened the rest of Bob's gifts and showed them to him. He slept most of the day, and then was up an hour or so, after dinner. While the girls and I got dinner, Rae sat beside him. I heard them talking and she was crying. They talked for about fifteen minutes then I heard him tell her it would be all right. Later he told me that he shared with her he was going to be with the Lord and he did not want her to worry. I could see a softening in his heart towards his mother I had never seen before. Since she was not a believer, I was proud of him for sharing his faith with her.

I asked Bob if he was ready to go and if he was fearful? He said he was a little afraid at times but that he had a peace about it. I praised God for taking Bob's fear away. We had a wonderful Christmas.

The day after Christmas, the children left. The hospice nurse came to say goodbye, as she was leaving on vacation for a week and felt she probably would not be seeing Bob again. It was good to see the bond that had formed between them. In the evening, Clay came back to stay the night, which I appreciated.

The next afternoon our good friends, Art and Evelyn, came to visit, Art stayed with Bob while Evelyn and I walked up to the cemetery. I wanted to show her the plot we had picked for our final resting place. When Evelyn saw the plot, she broke down and cried. I kept forgetting how hard it was on our close friends and family, especially those who did not see Bob regressing daily. I was faced with

Bob's rapid decline and the Lord continued to strengthen me daily. Evelyn and I talked about purchasing a memorial bench in Stanley Park,where Bob and I had spent so much time together.

Later, I discussed the idea with Bob about purchasing a memorial bench with his name inscribed on it. He declined because it would be too expensive. As he had a small life insurance fund, I knew I could cover the cost of the bench. I asked him, if money were not an issue, would he like to have a bench with his name on it. He said 'of course' but did not want me to spend the money. I was deeply touched by his thoughtfulness towards me.

Prior to the funeral, family and close friends decided as a memorial to Bob, they would contribute to the bench, instead of sending flowers. Flowers last a short time but the memorial bench would be there for a lifetime. In God's goodness, the contributions completely covered the cost of the bench.

By Thursday, December 29th, I was at the breaking point. I was up at seven am to give Bob his medication. He had been pacing for hours, and was in and out of my bed as well as his hospital bed in the living room, so neither of us were able to get any sleep. Looking back, I can see the combination of all the medication, the grief and sorrow of leaving his family, and the fear that comes with the dying process, were all taking a toll on him as well.

After I gave Bob his medication, I went back to bed and prayed for strength. I cried out to the Lord. I knew this should not be about me but in my exhaustion, it was! I had a good cry. I was mad at Bob for depending on me for spiritual answers when I didn't have those answers. The Lord was the only one who could help him, I couldn't help. Then I went from being mad at Bob to being really angry at God for not taking him, as after all, he had the power to end his suffering. Why was God putting our family through such pain? Why must Bob suffer? I never saw Bob turn to the Lord when he was well, so why would I expect him to do it now?. Then the Lord reminded me of how Bob had been turning to Him, in his own way. Of course he had. I prayed, "Forgive me Lord for my meltdown, I need your help so badly. I am losing it!!" Right away, I felt the Lord's presence calming me down. I said, "Thank you Lord for the peace you give when I think I can't go on." I got up, pulled myself together, and went to the living room to be with Bob.

CHAPTER 17

The next week another hospice nurse came by at two pm since our regular nurse was still on vacation. By that time, I was crying again. I cried most of the day, trying to hold back the tears so Bob would not see me. I did not want him to feel worse, and I could no longer bear to see him suffering. The nurse changed his medication and he slept well all afternoon.

New Years Eve, Art and Evelyn, our children, and Rae came to spend the evening. We played cards until midnight. However, Bob was not able to participate and slept most of the time. New Years day was also difficult. We were all near tears, as this would most likely be our last holiday with Bob. Rae asked me to come to sit by her. She wanted to know about the Lord, and where Bob was going. She had many questions. I had been praying for Rae to accept the Lord for many years, and now her heart was open. I thanked the Lord for the boldness he gave me once again to share Jesus. I gave her the little book 'Within Heavens Gates', which is a story of one woman's vision of Heaven and Rae said she would read it. I told her of the importance of receiving

Christ's sacrifice on the cross for our sins, so we could all be in Heaven together one day. I quietly prayed to myself that Rae would receive Christ, as her Savior.

Monday, January 2nd, was my 49th birthday. Our kids went out of their way to make it very special. They bought baby red roses and helped Bob sign my card. It broke my heart to see his signature so uneven and scratchy. He was the one with beautiful handwriting, and now it was worse than mine. The reality of seeing how weak he had become as the cancer had overtaken him was almost unbearable.

The next nurse's visit, we told her that Bob had fallen on the floor when he tried to get out of bed the night before. It was scary for all of us. We helped him back to bed. The nurse said, that because he was so weak she didn't want him getting out of bed anymore. So, the decision was made to put up the rails on the side of the bed. This was difficult for Bob as he had always been so self sufficient. He couldn't understand why he couldn't get up anymore. Another stage in the dying process!.

Mike stayed overnight, in case we needed him. Bob woke up several times because he had slipped down in the bed. It took both Mike and I to raise him up higher. We were on opposite sides of him trying to use the sheet under him to pull him up. It was a real challenge. We tried to be careful, but it was awkward. Bob was rambling, and some of his words we could not understand. He still had his sense of humor though, and said very clearly, "You guys make terrible nurses. " We all laughed.

The next day, the hospice volunteer gave Bob a bath. Afterwards, he was very relaxed and slept soundly. Rae paid for an overnight nurse to come from eleven pm to seven am, so I was able to return to my own bed and get some sleep. For the first time in a long time I was able to sleep all night without interruption. When I got up in the morning, the nurse had changed Bob's bed and bathed him. The overnight nurse was a Godsend and I was so grateful to Rae for her gracious contribution.

Bob's relationship with his mother had never been good. She divorced when he was two years old and remarried when he was eight. Bob became a rebellious teenager and was sent back and forth from his mom, to his birth father and his several wives. Bob was living on his own by the time he was seventeen years old. Rae had remarried again and tended to be possessive and domineering, according to Bob.

Through the years it had been difficult for me because when Rae could not get attention from Bob she would turn to me. She called me every day for comfort, and for the relationship she was looking for with her son. Daily Rae would come to our home arriving for lunch. This was stressful for both of us. I felt like I was caught in the middle, as each of them would share with me their complaints about the other.

By the time Bob was diagnosed with cancer, Rae was a widow, so her whole focus was on him. She wanted to be with him all the time and he did not want her around. I felt sorry for her, as I could only imagine what it would be like to lose a child, especially an only child.

As Bob and I had been in counseling over the years concerning family issues, we also discussed his mother. Our counselor advised that when Rae was upsetting us, to quietly bless her, saying to ourselves, "I bless you, Mom." We found that worked very well. While it didn't change what was going on, it seemed to diffuse the situation and I can see now it brought the added blessing of changing our attitude towards her.

Once, after a visit at her home, Bob said to me, "I blessed her six times." Another time, after he became bedridden, Bob was sitting up in bed when Rae came to visit and she was crying as she tried to talk to him. I was sitting in the dining room but could see him. He looked at me smiling, with four fingers raised. We both knew he was saying, "I blessed her four times." He was always so restless after her visits it often took an hour to settle him down. I felt so helpless. Of course she wanted to be there with him. I could not tell her not to come and yet, it upset him so much, and that was not good for him either. After her visits, I would sit with Bob, holding his hand, telling him how much I loved him, and I would try to calm him.

Rae's nieces, Joan and Sharon, came to stay with Rae during this time, and that was such a help for all of us. They brought her to see Bob, and took her home, when it was time for her to leave. Of course, she wanted to be with him every day, all day, but that was not good for anyone. Once, when she visited, Bob became extremely agitated and restless. He kept trying to turn away from her. He put his arm over his face and said to me, "get her out of here." I could not take the stress of it any longer and completely fell apart. I went to my room and lay across my bed, crying my heart out. Later I talked to the doctor, and told him the situation. He said to let her come twice a day for only fifteen minutes. I felt badly having to tell her this news but I was so thankful the doctor had taken control. I could not have done it on my own. As death drew nearer, I tried to leave them to have their visits without interference, hoping they would resolve their issues.

I called the hospice social worker, and told her of the stress we were under, and what the doctor had advised. I asked if she would go and see Rae to help her through this difficult time. At this point, Bob had not spoken coherently for several days and when I went into the living room, his eyes were fixed on me. He was smiling. Obviously, he had been listening to my conversation. I said, "You know exactly what is going on, don't you?" He kept smiling and I could see he was relieved that someone had taken control of the situation with his mother.

It appeared the Social worker must have also talked with Rae about releasing Bob, and letting him go, because the next time she came, she seemed more at peace and Bob was not so restless. I prayed that they had sorted out their differences, and said their goodbyes. One of the things I learned from this experience with them, is the importance of reconciling with loved ones while you still have the chance, as it is too painful for all involved if there are unresolved conflicts.

On January 9th, we were giving Bob morphine every four hours to keep him comfortable. He was sleeping most of the time now, too weak to respond. The nurse informed us that hearing, is the last of our senses to go, and he could probably still hear us, so I kept telling him I loved him. I reached over and took his hand, and as he had not spoken in several days I was shocked when he said as plain as day, "I'm all right, Hon." I answered, "I love you honey." Then he tried to lift himself up, straining to get his head off the pillow so he could be closer to me. He thrust his chin forward, the veins in his neck protruding as he stretched out his hand toward me, and with all the strength he could muster, in a husky voice said, "I love you, baby." Then he collapsed back onto the pillow. Those were the last words Bob ever spoke. As I continue to treasure and hold those words in my heart, I realized Bob and God could not have given me a better gift. Again I said, "I love you, and soon you will be with the Lord."

All our children came on January 10th, and decided to stay until Bob died, as he was now slipping in and out of consciousness. We took turns by his bedside, holding his hand, and reassuring him of how much we loved him. The hospice nurse was back from her vacation and was amazed he was still alive. She thought from his vital signs he would die that day, or the next. She told us with some patients they needed to be reassured that it is okay to let go. So I said, "Bob it's okay to let go, to be with the Lord. When you see him, be sure to come back and tell us before you go!"

We had heard stories of people having visions of the Lord before they died. When Bob's step-dad Pete was dying, he came out of his coma and said he was seeing the Lord. I was holding Pete's hand when all of a sudden he tried to lift his head and said, "Pat, the Lord is standing right here, wanting to take me with him." Pete's son John was with me and asked, "Who is he talking to?" I said, "He is talking to the Lord, John, why don't you take his other hand."

I knew Pete believed in God, but he told me he did not feel he needed Jesus in his heart. He thought all that 'Jesus stuff' was a bit fanatical. We had talked about the Lord a few times over the years and he said he believed in God, and that was enough. Pete had always said God, never using the word, Lord. So when he said the Lord was standing there I knew he meant Jesus. I was a new Christian at the time and never having experienced anything like this before, I did not know what to say, so I commented, "Really Pete? Why don't you talk to Him then?" The floodgates opened wide, and he said, "Oh I love you Lord. I want to be with you Lord." Then he went back into the coma and died shortly after. When it was over, my heart was filled so full I could not contain the tears of joy that were flowing. I was so grateful to the Lord for allowing me to be part of Pete's homecoming. What a privilege! John came and hugged me and said, "Nobody can take this away from us." He must have felt the awe of the moment, like I did.

So now, the children and I were hoping we could experience the miracle of Bob seeing Jesus before he died, as well. At one point Jennie said, "I wish we could know for sure where he was going." I think that may be the way it is at times for all of us, when it comes right down to dying. We know we go immediately to be with the Lord, as it says in 2 Corinthians 5:8, but if Bob were to come and tell us he saw Jesus, it would have been a great comfort to us all.

One evening when we were all together in the den, Clay was with Bob and suddenly came running into the den to get us. He said if we wanted to see our miracle, we had better come now, because Bob was talking to someone.

Clay had been with him when Bob said, "yes" and "uh uh", (meaning no) as plain as day. Bob did not say any more when we were with him, but he looked peaceful, and was breathing easier.

As Bob was no longer coherent, it was a comfort for me to have our children with us. There were times of laughter, and times of tears, as we reminisced about things that had happened over the years. It was good for all of us to be together. A year or so earlier, Bob had encouraged me not to worry, because we had good kids and they would be there for me. Now it had become true.

CHAPTER 18

I was talking to the Lord constantly, feeling His presence every step of the way. I could never have made it without Him and I was hoping everyone else felt the same way.

I experienced such peace as I sat by Bob's bedside, feeling I was a part of ushering him into the Kingdom. I thanked the Lord, for, "His peace that surpasses all understanding". The rest of the evening, I held Bob's hand, stroking his arms, and telling him to relax. I added that we loved him and we would be all right.

I had a good five and a half hours sleep as the nurse attended Bob through the night. He seemed relatively comfortable in the morning, however, he had a lot of mucus in his throat and was coughing. It sounded awful and it was pretty scary to hear. The nurse shared that it was harder on us, than on Bob. I hoped she was right.

The nurse noticed Bob was not 'letting go' and she suggested we call in our minister. In her opinion, she felt most people would have slipped away days ago. I called our counselor, who was also a pastor. He came and spent time with Bob, reassuring him of how much God loved him, and telling him it was okay to go. I left them alone and later he told me he prayed with Bob and read John, Chapter fourteen, to him.

Bob had not eaten or had anything to drink for over two weeks, and he was not looking good. He had lost so much weight that he was just skin and bones. His breathing was labored. At times, he would take a deep breath with a long pause in between, then his breath would become rapid and shallow, like he was running a race. When the nurse arrived she took Bob's vitals and his blood pressure was 64/32, his body was shutting down and she thought he would not last the afternoon.

We were all under so much stress, and we were exhausted. Suddenly, one of our children lashed out in a loud voice, "WHEN IS HE GOING TO DIE!!" We were shocked at the outburst, but then I realized we were all thinking the same thing but could not say it out loud. I answered, "I don't know honey, I am sure your dad is thinking the very same thing." If Bob heard what was said I figured he would be smiling and adding, "Yes, let's get on with it." He had always loved how this child was so outspoken and always said what was on her mind. I felt it was time for the kids to go back to their jobs and lead normal lives, however, we did not discuss it so all of them stayed except for Patti. She had to return to work. I was proud of how our children were walking through the process of their father's death.

I remember sitting at Bob's bedside, holding his hand, afraid to leave even to use the restroom in case he died while I was away. I knew I would be so angry with God if He took him when I was not by his side. Bob and I had walked this path together from the very beginning and I wanted to be with him at the finish. I realized my attitude was wrong and I was causing myself unnecessary stress, (besides I had to use the restroom). I confessed to the Lord I was trying to call the shots and if He saw fit to take Bob when I was not at his side I would be okay with that. Can you imagine? I was telling the God of the Universe, He could do things His way, as if I had any say in the matter. Once I released control, it was a huge relief. The next day I felt so much better about leaving Bob's side.

By now Bob had been in a coma for a couple of days. When the nurse came she turned Bob on his back and he started making noises like he was in pain. She assured us he was just clearing his throat, but it sounded like he was choking. We began crying, so she turned him on his side again. He then seemed more comfortable. When the nurse turned him back, Bob stopped breathing, and we thought he had died. But he soon began breathing again. The nurse bathed him and after she left, Bob's breathing became more rapid. His fingernails were blue and his hands were cold and clammy, and for his sake I was hoping the Lord would take him today. I was thankful to the Lord that Bob did not seem to be in any pain or discomfort. I spent the evening, holding his hand and telling him how much God and I loved him.

I went to bed around ten pm. I was sleeping on the floor by Bob's bed. Suddenly, I awoke with a start. I had heard Bob take a loud breath. I got up and took his hand and he then took a short quiet little breath that sounded like a puff of air being released. That was his last breath. He had gone to be with the Lord. I looked at the clock, it was one- twenty-nine am January 14, 1989. I thanked the Lord, for honoring my wishes; allowing me to be with him, and to be holding Bob's hand when he took his last breath and left this world. I felt like I was enveloped in a soft cocoon, surrounded by the Lord's presence, completely in awe. What a merciful, and gracious God we have.

After kissing Bob on the cheek and spending some time saying my goodbyes, I woke the children to tell them their dad was with the Lord. Patti had returned to Seattle to work so we called her and we also called Rae, to let her know he had passed. Bob's cousin Joan brought her right over to be with us. We kept Bob with us for a couple of hours until Patti arrived so she could spend some time saying goodbye. It was obvious Bob's spirit had left and although his body was there, he was no longer in the room.

We felt so many emotions- mainly relief that Bob was now with the Lord, and yet sorrow, that he would no longer be with us. We could feel the Lord upholding us. It was such a precious time as we reminisced about Bob and shared our fond memories. When we felt we were ready, we called the funeral home around 4:30 am. We then called our pastor Jeff, and he came to be with us.

We lived on the second floor of our building, and when the stretcher was brought up to get Bob, pastor Jeff said that I probably should not watch so I went into the den to be with the kids. When they wheeled Bob out I went back into the entry hall, and as I heard the stretcher going bump, bump, bump, down the stairs, the enormity of my loss hit me like a ton of bricks; I knew it was over and I would never see Bob again this side of heaven.

Deep wells of sorrow opened up in me and the pain was so great I began to wail. Pastor Jeff was holding me and telling me to let go. I had bottled up the tears for so long, they had to be released. The first sound that came out of my mouth seemed to give our children permission to let go as well. We all wailed at the same time. I remember feeling shocked at the crescendo coming with such force from the den as our children went to the depth of their pain, grieving the loss of their father. We sounded like a pack of wounded animals, I had never heard, or felt such pain. I am sure the whole condo complex knew Bob had died. As the initial pain subsided, we returned to sharing some of the good times. We were relieved that it was finally over for Bob, and he was out of his pain and misery.

Bob and I at 30 years together

Even though it was early, Pastor Jeff and Jennie's husband Todd, made us bacon and eggs for breakfast. It felt good to be taken care of and I think they were glad to be able to do something for us. Pastor Jeff left at six am and we all went back to bed. However, I was unable to sleep. Later that morning Clay took me to the funeral home to make the final arrangements.

As I was preparing to go to the funeral home, I was bending over the sink, washing my face, when I heard in my thoughts, "Well done, my faithful servant." I wondered if that could be the Lord? I began to hear singing, and then I realized I was the one singing, "Count your blessings name them one by one, count your many blessings see what God has done." I could not believe it! God gave me the song 'Count Your Blessings' when my husband had just died. I knew the Lord was trying to send me a message. I felt His presence with me, and it was a comfort. By giving me that song, I felt God was telling me, in the days ahead, I would need to keep my focus on Him, counting my blessings and not be consumed by my loss. That way I could stay strong.

The next day, Jennie and I ordered flowers and took Bob's artwork to be framed. His paintings were beautiful, and we planned to display them at the memorial service. Many of his friends did not even know he had been painting.

That evening, my sisters Karin and Jean, came down from British Columbia and took me to dinner. The ladies from my church had brought food so the kids took some, and went to be with Bob's mom. I was home by eight pm and our friends, Shar and Jim, stopped by for a short visit. After they left, I went to bed and had a good deep sleep. The next day, the kids left and I looked forward to having the days to myself. We had been living in such close quarters for so long, and under such stress, we all needed some space. Since I was not ready to be alone all night, I was grateful when Mike came to stay during the nights. Once again, I felt the goodness of the Lord, and my children.

For the next few days friends stopped by to give their condolences. The church sent food over for the following two weeks. Tuesday, January 17th, was the memorial service. The kids came at noon. We were all holding up pretty well. I did not want to start talking about memories of Bob right then, because I was holding back tears and did not want to fall apart before the service.

So many people attended, that there was standing room only. The funeral home put some of Bob's paintings at the front, among the flower arrangements. It looked so beautiful, it was almost like an art show. It was when I saw how lovely everything looked, that I began to fall apart. Our good friend Jim Eney, and pastor Jeff, did an excellent job of conducting the service. Some of the things they shared, were the wonderful, romantic things Bob used to do for me on special occasions. The husband of one of Patti's friends sang "The Lord's Prayer" and, "It is Well With My Soul." I wanted, "It is Well With My Soul" sung, because even though it was terribly difficult, everything WAS well with my soul. I knew Bob was now with the Lord.

During the time of sharing, it blessed my heart to hear so many people get up and say what Bob had meant to them over the years. I wished Bob could have been there to hear the wonderful things that were said about him, but I thought he probably was there, in spirit. It was truly an uplifting service. Afterwards, we had a reception in the back of the sanctuary. I greeted family and friends, and many people I did not know, but they all loved Bob and wished our family well.

When the service was over, our good friends Cathy, and Sal Lo Grande, invited our family to their home for a more intimate reception. It was a good time, but I was exhausted when it was over. I appreciated that Patti and Jennie stayed with me that night as I was not yet ready to be alone.

ADJUSTING TO DEATH

The Lord says, I will guide you along
the best pathway for your life.
I will advise you and watch over you.

Psalm 32:8 from The Living Bible

CHAPTER 19

Jennie stayed with me as I began to adjust to Bob's death and being alone. She helped me while I made some business calls, notifying different companies of Bob's death. When it was time for her to leave, I sensed how hard it was for her to go, but I assured her I would be all right. I had dinner, thanks to the church, paid some bills and in the evening I wrote some thank you notes. I began to feel the loss of Bob. I was not crying, but I did feel physical pain in my chest. I re-read my devotional, "Streams In The Desert", and was comforted as the readings over the last few days were reminding me that The Lord is in control, goes before me, and will never leave me, or forsake me.

My cat Boots and I went to bed about 11:30 in the evening. I slept well even though I woke up several times during the night, but each time I would fall right back to sleep. I slept until 8 in the morning and woke up feeling completely rested and relaxed. There was no fear in me whatsoever, and that was truly a miracle. All my life I had been afraid to stay alone at night. Even as a little girl I was afraid of the dark. Years ago, when Bob would stay out late and sometimes all night, I would be afraid, even though I had the kids at home. I would wonder what I would do if something happened. At that time I was not driving, so I felt the full responsibility for my small children on my shoulders, and I was terrified by that responsibility.

When we bought the Condo, we knew I would eventually live there alone. When we were viewing it to buy, I felt safe as soon as I walked in the door. There were units on both sides of us, above and below, so I knew there would be people around if I needed help. That might sound strange to some, but it was very important and real to me. When I went to bed the first night I was alone, I prayed for God's protection and peace, and He came through for me. God had always been so good to me and kept His promises.

Sometime later, I went with a friend to Stanley Park to pick out the memorial bench for Bob. After looking at many, we found the perfect bench right across from the Parks Board office at the south entrance of the park. Bob and I had sat on that bench many times, looking across the water and enjoying the sunsets. We went back to the Park's Board office, and the man in charge came with us, looked at the bench we had chosen, and said it was available. I was excited and felt incredible peace. I knew without a doubt this was the right bench.

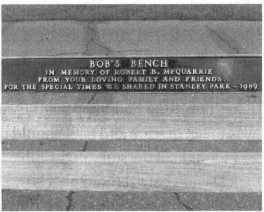

I talked to Bob and said, "I know you would love it, I miss you, and wish you were here to share this with me. But I guess if you were here, I wouldn't be doing this would I?" Once home, I looked over the cards that had arrived in the mail. I was overwhelmed with people's kindness.

During this time, I was not sleeping well. I wasn't afraid but I woke up every couple of hours. I was unable to focus and could not get motivated during the day. I walked around as though I was in a daze. I knew there was much that I should be doing, but I just could not seem to accomplish anything, I felt lost. I knew exercise would help me, and even though I had a stationary bike in my room, I had to force myself to ride it. I felt like I had to set my will in motion to make myself do anything. I did not feel weepy, I just listless, and numb. It all seemed like a bad dream.

In the days that followed the funeral, my friends surrounded me with company and comfort. Later, I realized how important it was to spend some time each day with others, as the evenings were more than enough time alone. I was still dazed and not able to feel my emotions. I asked

the Lord,"Is this wrong? Where are the tears and weeping?"
I was so relieved that Bob was out of pain and with the
Lord. I was sad and lonely on the inside and yet I knew my
grief was not showing outwardly. I could laugh, and talk as
though nothing had happened. I was almost embarrassed
by my lack of tears and felt I should be reacting differently".

I thought of the story in the Bible in 2 Samual, where God
took David's baby. I thought of how David wept, prayed, and
fasted while the baby was with him and then as soon as the
baby died, he got up, dressed, ate, and returned to normal
life. I felt like that was similar to what was happening with
me. A lot of mourning took place while Bob was alive, and
life had been on hold for both of us. I wondered, now that
he was gone, was it time to start living again? It was so
confusing. I realized I needed to accept how I was feeling
and not try to figure out if it was right or wrong.

CHAPTER 20

O ne day, the hospice nurse stopped by and told me about a group that met weekly called P.A.L, the acronym stood for, Positive Approach to Loss, and was a place for people to share their grief over losing a loved one. I was interested enough to attend a meeting, so a few weeks later I went. However, it was difficult on days when I was having a good day, to listen to other people's pain. People in the group were all at different stages of grief. It seemed to hurt me, more than to help me, so after going for a few weeks I decided no longer to attend.

It was now the end of January, and almost two weeks since Bob's memorial. I missed him. I felt like the dam was about to break wide open, and there was such an ache in my heart. I loved him so much, and it was hard to believe he was gone. I was getting over the shock of the last few weeks when he had been so sick. I felt such relief when Bob went to be with the Lord, but now my constant companion, was loneliness.

As I was sitting on the couch in the living room having a good cry, deep gut wrenching sobs came from the depths of my being. Poor Boots, did not know what to do, so he jumped up on my lap, and sprawled out on my chest frantically purring. He stroked my cheeks with his paws trying to comfort me. That made me cry harder, as I hugged him close. I don't know how I would have made it without Boots, he would become such a comfort to me in the years ahead.

The day after my cry, I felt so much better. Up to this point, I had felt like I was in a cocoon and disconnected from my emotions. I felt like I could comfort others, who were also grieving over Bob, and not go to pieces. I was beginning to worry about my lack of emotion, but after my cry I did not feel as though I were in such a daze. I thanked the Lord for His peace.

One evening, Clay came and took me to dinner and then out to play Bingo at a hall in Ferndale. I had enjoyed playing Bingo when I was young, at the community hall in the town where I grew up. In those days, someone called out the numbers, and if we had them on our card we covered them with buttons. As we played the game, we laughed and talked with each other and had a lot of fun. I learned immediately that bingo had changed over the years, and had become serious business. Some people played two or three cards and stamps were used instead of buttons! It was fast paced, and Heaven help you if you even looked at your neighbor, let alone talked to them. Clay thought I might enjoy going once a week, thinking it would help with the loneliness. I appreciated his thoughtfulness and how he was trying to help but as I was seeking companionship, I didn't think Bingo would be high on my priority list. After taking me home, Clay spent the night, for which I was grateful.

I could see Rae, also needed someone right now, so I was spending a lot of time taking her to lunch and having her come over in the evening. She often called for me to come along with her to the cemetery. Rae visited the cemetery every day, and I remembered Bob saying he did not want us sitting at his grave so I often declined. Rae was forgetful and when we would get together, she would go over every detail of Bob's cancer, his death, and the funeral, asking me to relive every detail with her. At times I could hardly bear going over it again and again. I finally pretended I could not remember and tried to change the subject.

As the days went by, my children and friends continued to be faithful, still calling and coming over for a visit. I was getting back into my exercise routine, and feeling better for it. However, at times I still had to force myself to exercise. Having a routine helped fill the long lonely hours. I recognized a lot of what I was doing was just busyness to help me get through the day. I was missing Bob so much but I was thankful he was with the Lord. Sometimes, when I wished he was here I had such a painful ache in my heart. I would not actually call it loneliness, but more like a sense of emptiness, or loss. The Bible says in Mark 10:8 NIV "and the two will become one flesh, so they are no longer two but one." I knew that to be true, as I felt like part of me had been ripped away.

In Mid February, Mike and Janelle came and picked up Boots, because I was going to Jennie's to spend a few days over Valentine's. As Jennie and I were visiting she showed some pictures she had taken at Christmas. We cried as we saw Bob in his hospital bed, looking so thin and haggard. She told me about a dream she had; that two men had broken into their house in the night and were walking down the hall toward the bedroom talking to each other. Then she woke up. A few days later she had the same dream, only this time one of the men came into the bedroom and sat down beside her on the bed. He said, "Don't worry Jennie, I am all right". Then he left and she woke up. She said to me; "Mom, it was dad! I couldn't believe it. He was so full of energy. I couldn't get over his eyes, they were full of light and glowing, and his face was radiant, he looked so happy."

Jennie shared that she was not scared and said the dream was so real. She said, "I know he was there because my cat was sleeping on my pillow and was standing up with its back arched, hair standing on end, freaking out." I thought it was gracious of the Lord as I remembered when her dad was dying she was the one who said "I wish we could know for sure where he was going and that he would be all right."

When Patti had been visiting recently, she said she also had a dream. She could not remember what she was doing but said, "Dad was just standing there in the background, not saying anything." She added, "I felt like he was watching over us." Even though we did not know what to think of these dreams they were a real comfort to us.

When Patti and Jennie shared their dreams with me, I have to admit, even though I was so happy they had both seen Bob, I was a little sad that I did not have that same joyful experience. I told them the grief group I had visited, said it was perfectly normal to dream about a loved one who was gone. We all felt Jennie's experience was more like a heavenly visitation, than an ordinary dream.

In the last years of our marriage, Bob had always acknowledged holidays in some special way, with flowers, gifts or dinners. Since I was at Jennie and Todd's over this Valentine's Day, Clay came over with flowers and Jennie, Patti and Mike brought me wonderful cards and a box of heart shaped chocolates. I thanked God for my children helping to make my first Valentine's day without Bob so special. After our Valentine's Day celebration, I left Jennies and cried all the way home, knowing when I got there the house would be empty. I had been doing that a lot lately, knowing I could cry and wail loudly in the car and no one would hear me. Sometimes I cried and no tears would come, just a pain in my chest and stomach. It felt like I was sobbing on the inside, shaking and contracting my stomach muscles. I hated it when that happened because at least with tears there was a release, but with the dry cries, as I called them, the pain stayed with me. When I got home I felt Bob's presence and it was such a comfort. Mike brought my cat Boots back later which was also a comfort, our pets are such companions to us. God seems to have given them a gift of sensing what our needs are and being able to reach into the innermost parts of our hearts.

Later that week, I heard from a friend that her husband had sent her flowers on Valentine's Day and he had written on her card to be ready at a certain time as he was surprising her with a romantic dinner. She said he had never done anything like that before so we both knew it was a direct result of the pastor sharing at Bob's memorial what he used to do for me. Another young man Bob worked with called and shared with me some hard things he was going through in his life, he said he visited Bob's grave many times and talked to him. He knew Bob was a Christian and said he felt peace when he was at Bob's grave. As my friends told me their stories my heart was deeply touched. I hope Bob knows how much he had influenced his friends and others. I thanked the Lord that He was using Bob even after his death.

CHAPTER 21

It had been a month since Bob's memorial. In the morning when I awoke I felt different, somehow lighter and I hoped it would last. There was not as much physical pain. I felt like the grief was no longer so attached to me. The pain had been such a heavy, crushing feeling, as I missed Bob so much. I still thought of him, but the thoughts came less frequently. Before, the pain was constant and I almost felt guilty that I was not experiencing it all the time now. I decided this must be a normal part of the grieving process.

I began to wonder if it would be helpful to find a job. If there was somewhere I had to be each day, at least I would have a purpose when I got up in the morning. I saw that La Parfumerie, a retail fragrance/Beauty Salon, was advertizing for a makeup artist/retail clerk. At the time I was a licensed esthetition, so I applied. I informed the owner that my husband had died a month earlier and I wasn't sure if I was ready to go back to work. He assured me it was a low stress job. A few days later he called and wanted me to come in and meet his wife, since they worked together in the store. The interview went well, and I started work on March 16, 1989, almost two months to the day that Bob died.

I still was not sure if I was ready, but felt it would be good for me to try to go to work. I was happy that I had been honest with the owners about how I was feeling. I enjoyed the job, for the most part, but found it hard to retain the names of all the products and perfumes they sold. It didn't feel like my brain was working to its full potential. Most days went well, but as time went on, I dreaded going in to work because I felt I had to stifle myself when I wanted to sit and have a good cry. I was still missing Bob terribly. Occasionally, I did cry and my boss and his wife were always very kind, but more and more I felt as though I could not continue to work, as I realized I needed more time to grieve. I worked four months, before realizing I needed to give my notice, and though the owners were very kind, they were disappointed to lose me. I appreciated my time there, but was glad it was over, realizing it was too soon for me to have a job.

Since the stages of grief do not always follow a set pattern, I found myself back in unbearable pain. At times, the days were difficult, I had trouble sleeping, and coping with everyday life. I wondered if I was depressed? Missing Bob was sweeping over me in painful waves. I loved to wear his sweatshirt around the house, it felt like his arms were wrapped around me. His scent was still on his clothing, so I kept his clothing in the closet next to mine.

By the end of April, I knew it was time to go through his things and send them off to the Salvation Army. Mike and Clay had come earlier to take whatever they wanted of their dad's things. I felt badly giving Bob's clothes away as he had some really nice things. I would have liked to see them go to someone I knew. But Jeff, our pastor, said by sending them to the Salvation Army they went to the working poor, people who had a need but could not afford new things. I felt better, knowing Bob's clothing would be a blessing to someone. I boxed up all his things, put them in the entry hall, and called for the truck to come and pick them up. I was feeling good by then about giving them away, and when the man came to get them he said, "Oh, are you doing spring cleaning?" I said "No, my husband had died and these are his things." Again the grief swept over me like a flood and I started to cry. The poor man was so flustered he didn't know what to do. He said, "Oh, It's okay maam. You're young. You'll find another man." This comment struck me funny, and if I was not hurting so badly I would have laughed. I thought the last thing I wanted was another man. I wanted Bob! This was just another experience in the long journey of grief!

CHAPTER 22

In May, I began going through a whole new stage in the grieving process. Anger! I remember one awful night around the end of the month, I cried myself to sleep, dredging up stuff from the past that I thought I had already processed. I was amazed at the intensity of my emotions. I had forgiven Bob for all the past pain and hurt he had caused me. At least, I had said the words. But, because we had never been able to talk through our conflicts together they were not resolved, and I had buried anger deep inside.

I was angry at Bob for all those years long ago, when I had to put up with his drinking, flirting and unfaithfulness. When I would confront him, he would deny it and say I was just being jealous. I now realize I was going through exactly what Bob went through with his mother, reliving unresolved issues. This was something I thought I had learned from them *not* to do.

At that time, I was golfing once a week with my friend Pat, who had known us since before we were married. She knew us well, and all Bob and I had been through together. Since Bob died, I had been enjoying the memories of our last few years and was now sharing with her the wonderful change I got to see in him. But then the anger came to the surface, and I shared some things that happened between us long ago. As we hit our golf balls, and walked along to take another shot, I ranted and raved along the way about his mistreatment of me. After a few holes like this, I guess she had enough, as she laughed and said, "I wondered when you were going to remember how it really was!" Because the final years for Bob and I were good, I had been putting him on a pedestal. People say that is often common when someone dies. I was sorry to say he *was not* on the pedestal at this stage of my grieving process!

As Mother's Day approached, I was apprehensive about how I would handle it without Bob. On the day before Mother's Day, my daughter-in-law, Janelle, took me to a mother/daughter fashion show. I appreciated her thoughtfulness, and we had a lovely time. On Mother's Day, the kids came to take me to dinner. I had been feeling lonely all day and fell into the trap of feeling sorry for myself. In the morning, as I left for church, I thought how nice it would have been if even one of my children had come with me, it would have meant so much. I remember thinking, "well I guess it is just you and me Lord. No one else really cares." I knew as soon as the thought came to me, that it was completely ridiculous and irrational.

I had always tried not to interfere in my kids lives, as they became adults. Now that I was alone, I did not want to be a clinging mother who expected her children to take care of her. I was happy they had their own lives and I tried to be respectful. I knew I needed to make a life for myself. I could not look to any human being for my happiness, and only the Lord could meet my deepest needs. I thanked the Lord for that thought, and asked Him to forgive me for my selfish temper tantrums earlier in the day. Even though I felt abandoned in the morning, attending church alone, I willed myself to be thankful my children were coming to take me to dinner. I hoped this anger stage would not last too long as it made me feel miserable and was not fair to others. I did not like my angry behavior and the way I felt. When the kids came they brought cards and gifts, and we had a lovely dinner together. I thanked them, and the Lord, for making this Mother's Day special.

In June the children and I decided it was time to scatter Bob's ashes. We each took turns scattering a few, and we shed tears as we said goodbye to Bob. It was difficult, but an important step in the healing process. I felt very close to Bob, and my kids, as we scattered his ashes together.

As time went on my days were filled with activities. It was a warm and sunny summer. I spent one day a week golfing, two or three days a week with Rae, as well as spending time having lunch with friends, and visiting my children. I drove to Birch Bay most afternoons, and lay on the beach until the sun went down, listening to praise and worship music. The healing love of Christ came and comforted me, as I cried and grieved for hours at a time.

In my loneliness, I was eating a lot of sweets and as I had always struggled with my weight it was scaring me. I got down to my goal weight a year or so before Bob died and I could feel myself putting the weight back on again. Bob and I used to play a game concerning how much I weighed.

I would not tell him, even though he would plead with me. I was embarrassed to tell him my heaviest weight. I was constantly dieting, and he would say, "What are you down to now, five hundred pounds?" I would say, "I wish," and we would laugh because we both knew I was nowhere near that weight.

Sometimes when I got on the scale, Bob would try to sneak up behind me and see the scale. Even though I had made it to my goal weight, he did not know what it was and he made me promise I would tell him before he died. I said I would. One day shortly after he died, I was sitting in a restaurant when I suddenly realized I had forgotten to tell him. The realization hit me like a ton of bricks. A feeling of shock went through my body and I almost went into hysterics. How could I have forgotten? I had promised I would tell him my weight before he died. I was so disappointed in myself, as telling him would have brought closure to our little game. I am sure he did not care or even think about it. We had a lot more on our minds at that time than my weight. How I wished I could have kept my promise to him and finished our little game. I know he would have loved it.

After the way I reacted to that memory, I could see how fragile my emotions were, and I cried all the way home. I felt the same physical pain in my chest, neck and head that had been so familiar after he died. I cried and cried. I missed him so much. Once again I was grateful for my car, where I could really let loose with my tears, and no one would hear me. It saved Boots a lot of stress too. I felt the Lord's presence, and thanked Him for how He comforted and supported me during those painful times. Those experiences were an important part of the process and the words my mother used to say came back to me, "This too shall pass"." I accepted those precious times of intense sorrow and grieving, because the Lord was so near to me.

There were days I could think of my life going on, either alone, or with another husband. The next day, I would be crying, missing Bob so much. I hoped these feelings were normal. I loved Bob and knew that I always would, although I did not feel the intensity of my love for him the same way every day. At times I would be angry that he was with the Lord and I was left by myself. I wished I could describe the pain and emptiness I felt, at times. Some days I felt like falling into the well of self pity and staying there, crying and feeling sorry for myself. Thankfully that was happening less, and less often.

CHAPTER 23

Just before the one year anniversary of Bob's death, as I was sitting in church one Sunday, I noticed a visitor; a man about my age was sitting in the row in front of me. I recognized him as a man I had met previously in another church that Bob and I had visited, and I knew he had lost his wife a couple of years earlier. I remember how I used to pray for him, knowing how hard it must have been for him to lose his wife, and knowing I was about to walk the same path. I wondered what he was doing at my church?

I thought of him off and on through the rest of the day. I loved Bob so much, I wondered how could I even be thinking of someone else so soon? It seemed right to wait a whole year before even thinking of another man, so I could complete the grieving process. At that time I was thinking the grieving process was only a year, not realizing everyone's process was different. I thought, "What would my kids think? What would the Lord think?" I felt terrible and asked the Lord to forgive me for being so fickle. I could not believe my thoughts, and hoped I would not see him again for a very long time, as it made me feel guilty, and nervous, to be thinking of him. I felt so vulnerable, as though I was robbing Bob of his time. I felt I should still be grieving for Bob, and not thinking of another man.

A couple of months later, I received a card in the mail from the man I saw at church. Not to give away his real name, I will call him 'Bill'. He asked me if I would like to go for coffee. I freaked out. I praised the Lord because he was such a nice Christian man, but then I spent the day crying. What a basket case! I never knew an invitation for coffee could trigger so many emotions. I still was not ready to date, and I knew it. I wanted to go out with Bill, as I missed a man's company, but I was scared to death. I missed being held by Bob and knew I was vulnerable.

After praying for a few days, I wrote to Bill and told him I did not feel I was ready to see anyone, even for coffee. He called and was very understanding and thanked me for being honest. He was a very nice man, and as we talked for about forty minutes, I lost all my fear and fantasies about him. I could see a nice friendship, but nothing more. What a relief! How silly I was to get myself all worked up.

I noticed I had been over-reacting a lot since Bob died. Bob had only been gone a short time and yet I could feel myself pulling away from him, and getting on with my life. I now had longer periods of time between thoughts of Bob. The pain would now come only periodically and yet, I felt like it should have been there all the time. I felt so sad. I knew Bob's memory would fade but I was not ready to let go of him. It scared me to think about how fast someone could pass out of one's life. When thoughts of Bob came, they no longer consumed me the way they had before. I had always enjoyed those thoughts, and felt comforted by them. However, I realized I was also thinking about Bill. I wished he would call me. Then when he called, I wished he didn't call, when he didn't call, I wanted to talk to him, how crazy was that? No wonder men have such a hard time understanding women!

I was torn between two emotions, hanging on to the old, and trying to move on to the new. I decided the only way to conquer my fear was to face it head on. I decided if 'Bill' called again, I would suggest we go for a drive as that felt safe to me. I thought if I got to know him I might be rid of all my confusing emotions. Once again I felt depressed and weepy. I did not like the range of emotions I was feeling. I wished I could plod along on an even keel and not feel much of anything. I just wanted to be numb again, and not be able to feel any strong emotions similar to those I felt when Bob first died. I wanted to continue enjoying Bob's memory, and feeling his comfort. I wanted to savor this time, but I also felt like I was being swept along into another stage that I was not ready for, or not willing to accept. Grieving is a strange process!

In July, Bill called again and asked if I would like to go for a drive. I thought it was interesting that he suggested we go for a drive when I had decided earlier that I would suggest the same thing. It had been three and a half months since I first talked to him, so I felt that he had been considerate in allowing me more time to grieve. He came that evening and we drove along Chuckanut Drive, to Anacortes. We talked mostly about our spouses, who had both died of cancer, and of what we were doing with our lives now.

He said he was happy being single, but would like to have someone in his life to take to dinner, and maybe to the theater occasionally, but, I was not sure if that was what I wanted. I kept comparing him to Bob, and I knew that was not fair.

I felt so fragile, like a wounded bird; vulnerable and weak. I was aware I needed more time to heal. He said he would call, and that maybe we could go out again. Even though I had mixed emotions, I said that would be nice. Making conversation and putting an effort into developing a new friendship was hard work. Because of these emotions, I felt like I had nothing to offer Bill. I shed many tears the next few nights, as I enjoyed the comfort of Bob's memory, and I did not want that to end. Bob and I had so many hard years, but the last few years had been good. I wondered if feeling this way was okay or if I was climbing into a shell, so I would not have to go out into the "real world" as my son so often said. I could see I needed to lighten up with this new 'dating stage', and not make it such a big deal. Bill and I had several phone conversations and during one of these conversations we decided to drive up to Mt. Baker. Even though he was a nice man, I felt this would be our last time together, and as it turned out, it was our last date.

A few days later, a friend called saying she had someone she wanted me to meet, and that he had lost his wife to cancer, so we had that in common. I met him, and we drove to Birch Bay. He confided in me he had lost his wife just three weeks earlier. Wow! I thought it was way to soon for him to be seeing someone. I felt he was trying to run from the pain, and I knew from experience he could not escape the grieving process. I could feel his pain, as he shared stories about his wife with me. The next day, a lovely bouquet of flowers were delivered to my door with a card saying how much he enjoyed our visit. We saw each other for a couple more times and during our last time together, I was feeling his pain so strongly, I realized that I was tapping into my own pain.

After we said goodbye, I went home and fell across my bed, sobbing hysterically. Then suddenly, I heard a key in the door. It was Mike, Janelle and Clay. I was so embarrassed to be caught sobbing. I told them I still missed their dad so much. They knew I had just come home from a date and Mike said, "Mom, don't go on dates if you don't want to." I said I did not know it would have this effect on me and be this painful. I felt sorry for my sons as they stood looking at me, laying across my bed, with pain on their faces, recognizing there was nothing they could do for me.

One morning I awoke with a strong feeling that it was time to remove my wedding rings. I was still a young woman, at fifty years old, and if I was going to be dating, it seemed I should not be wearing my rings. Wearing them made me feel I was being unfaithful to Bob, even though he had been gone over a year. This was one more stage in the healing process.

After the dating period, I felt restless, I could not sit still and wanted to do something different. I asked the Lord, "what is it you have in store for my life?" I had always been overly responsible, trying to do, and say, the right thing, and to be there for everyone. Lately, part of me wanted to do something completely 'off the wall' and impulsive. Some days I wanted to get in my car, and run away. Run, run, run!

I looked into the possibility of going to London to study for a year with a Community College. That would certainly be out of character for me. For one thing, I had never been to college and did not like studying when I was in school. Several days after thinking this new idea through, I finally came to my senses. Again I talked to the Lord, "Who can understand me? I can't even understand myself. You are the only one who knows me completely. How I praise you for being in my life, thank you for stopping me before I did something foolish." I felt so deeply, and with such intensity about everything, whether it was for the beauty of nature, the glorious colors of the sunset, my love for my family and friends or gratefulness for just being alive. I had always been an emotional person but the depth of my emotions surprised me. I wondered if it was grieving or whether I had I entered into the change of life, or if it was a little of both.

CHAPTER 24

As I entered into the stage of walking through life as a single, I talked to my counselor, who used to work for Burden Bearers, a Christian counseling organization in Seattle. He now had his own ministry in Bellingham. When we talked about my future he encouraged me to pursue a counseling career. I sent my resume' to the director of Burden Bearers in Abbotsford, B.C., and was called for an interview. Then I received a letter from my former pastor, telling me about a training session coming to Seattle with Larry Crabb, a Christian psychologist who had written many books on the subject of counseling. My pastor also encouraged me to follow up with Burden Bearers.

The area director for Young Life, gave me the name of a church in Burnaby, B.C., that had a two year training program in counseling. In September, I again had an interview with Burden Bearers Ministries. They were having a training session in November, and I was asked if I would be interested in facilitating a twelve step program, as they were thinking of putting together a hospice program. I felt the Lord was leading me into the area of counseling, and all the spiritual 'gifting tests' I had taken over the years, strongly pointed to counseling as my gift. This impacted me, as I sensed that the Lord was walking with me, opening the doors for a counseling career.

I was grateful to Bob for providing me with a new car, that was paid for, and as we had a small insurance policy, I didn't have to work right away and could take some time to train for counseling. I praised the Lord for providing for me so well. In November, I trained with Burden Bearers in Abbotsford. I loved studying topics like Birth Order, Affirmations, Self esteem, Stress, Depression, Anger, Spiritual Warfare, and Forgiveness, and how to help people stuck in these areas. I felt peace and joy being in the class. I loved the training, and felt like I had found my niche. I remembered as a young girl I had always been interested in how people thought, and why they behaved the way they did. From that time, I felt the Lord had given me the calling of counselor. There had been many sidetracks along the way but now a new phase had begun.

CHAPTER 25

The holidays were coming and a lot of memories were resurfacing. Going to church, singing hymns, and hearing Christmas music was very difficult for me.

Our family hadn't decided what we were going to do for Christmas. We all wanted to do something different than we usually did, as we knew how hard it would be without Bob. Christmas Eve was on a Sunday, so I went to church but had to leave as they sang the last hymn. I cried all the way home. My grief surfaced and I had to lie down on the bed, feeling depressed. Suddenly, I felt as though the Lord was wrapping his arms around me, and I felt His peace fill me. I felt so much better as the pain and tears were lifted from me. Later that evening, the children came and spent the night. We slept until eight-thirty am, Christmas morning.

Mike left and went over to pick up his girlfriend, Janelle so she could be with us. A few days before Christmas Eve, he shared he was planning to give her an engagement ring, and ask her to marry him. She agreed, and when they came back, we were all very excited. She shared that she had no idea she was getting a ring for Christmas.

I was happy for them because I loved her, and was glad she would be my daughter-in-law. As we opened our gifts I kept fighting back the tears. Bob had always handed out our gifts and made a big deal of saving my gift from him until last. I was anticipating that at the end of handing out our gifts there would be no gift from Bob. Thankfully, Clay took over Bob's role of handing out the gifts and I am sure it was hard for him. We all felt the loss of Bob, but we held ourselves together pretty well. I think the excitement of Mike and Janelle getting engaged helped us get through our first Christmas without Bob.

Later in the afternoon, we went to Coquitlam, B.C., to visit my parents. Then we headed over to our good friends, Art and Evelyn's place in Burnaby, for Christmas dinner. We returned home to Bellingham in the evening and everyone went home, except Clay, I was thankful when he spent the night so I would not be alone. My first Christmas without Bob was a good day, but I was thankful when it was over. I had always loved the decorating, baking, and Christmas music but I was too emotional and could not get into the spirit; in truth, I wished I could have skipped Christmas altogether. Christmas took on a whole new dimension for me that year, as I had a new empathy for those who were lonely and did not have their loved one with them to share the holidays. I thanked God that I had family and friends who were there for me, as I knew there were a lot of people who were completely alone.

I had promised my friend Carol, I would go with her to

her company Christmas party on Friday December 29th. She worked at Arco, and they were having their Christmas party at Crescent Beach, B.C. She said a lot of employees had worked on the pipeline from Alaska, through British Columbia, so there would be both Canadians and Americans attending the party. Carol said she was afraid she would get lost, and since I knew the area well, asked if I would go along. I was excited about having a party to go to, so we both got dressed up and were on our way. I jokingly said if there were a lot of boring speeches and I fell asleep, to wake me up when it was time to go home. We drove straight to the building and I noticed Clay's truck was in the parking lot. He had shared with me he was dating a new girl, and I thought maybe she worked at Arco. It would be fun to see the surprised look on his face when he saw me arrive. As we went up the stairs, I noticed there were no lights on, so I said to Carol, "I think we are in the wrong place. There does not seem to be anyone here." She ignored my comment, and kept leading me up the stairs. When we got to the door, I could see people in the dark, holding cameras up to their faces. I said, "We are at the wrong party, these people are waiting to surprise someone." Carol opened the door, and I said, "No we can't go in there. They are expecting someone else, and they will take our picture instead."

I thought we must have gotten the directions mixed up, these people will be the ones surprised when we walk in and we are not who they are expecting. I could not understand why Carol was not listening to me. She forged ahead and pushed me through the open door into what appeared to be a crowd of strangers. Suddenly, the lights came on, and they all yelled SURPRISE! I saw my sister and some of my friends, and wondered what they were all doing there? I was completely surprised. I remember that I said "what is this?" I could not figure out what was going on. My daughter Jennie, came up to me and said, "Happy Birthday mom." Then everyone started singing, "Happy Birthday". I could not believe it, a party for me?

I was caught by surprise because it was four days before my birthday. Of course, I felt the loss of Bob, strongly, as I stood there without him. I started to cry. Jennie wrapped her arms around me, and we both cried. What a wonderful surprise party! My knees were shaking so badly, I could hardly walk. I was completely speechless. About fifty family and friends had come to celebrate. My kids had planned it all and asked Carol to bring me. I was so grateful to my children and all who had come. I felt so cared for, and loved. It meant a lot to me that they had come to support me, since this was my first Birthday without Bob.

A few days later I was dreading New Year's Eve, but thankful to be spending it with our friends, Art and Evelyn. We went to dinner, and took the sky train downtown to Robson Square in Vancouver. The square was filled with hundreds of people celebrating, and listening to different bands playing their music. We decided to take the sky train home at about ten pm to beat the throngs of people who would be returning home after midnight. It was so much fun.

I still missed Bob but it was not as difficult as it was at Christmas. On the way home New Year's Day, I stopped and visited with Rae. She was still going over every detail of Bob's death, asking, "Pat, did Bob die of cancer?" Then, she wanted to relive every detail of his illness. I felt sorry for her and tried to be patient because I knew she was having difficulty with her memory, but it was so hard on me to keep going over the pain of Bob's death. The next day was January, 2nd, which was my actual birthday, I went shopping, and bought a new outfit, "Happy Birthday to me!". Since my kids had already blessed me with a marvelous surprise Birthday party, they all called to wish me a good day. It had been a good day.

CHAPTER 26

I decided to go to San Diego later in January to a 'Young Life Convention'. Bob and I had been involved with Young Life for several years before he got cancer and I thought it would be good for me to get away, and be involved with something outside myself. Whenever we traveled, Bob had always made the arrangements. I always followed along with him, thankful that he had taken care of all the details. This was my first trip alone, and I was scared to death.

I made the hotel reservation in San Diego, and arranged the flight from Bellingham. I mustered up all my courage and then was on my way. I transferred planes in Seattle, found my flight, and sat next to a woman who was going home to San Diego. We enjoyed each other's company and it made the trip go by quickly. We continued the friendship by phone, and letters, for several years.

When I arrived at the airport in San Diego, there was a mix up concerning my ride to the Marriott. We finally sorted it out and I arrived at the hotel, quite frazzled. When I went to the desk to check in, I found they didn't have my name on the register. The hotel was full, since there were

2400 guests registered for the convention. I started to panic, and could feel myself losing control. I felt embarrassed, and knew if I broke down crying, I wouldn't be able to stop. It took all my courage to make the trip by myself, now with things not going well, I was totally stressed.

The desk clerk sent me to another office and on the way there, I ran into (almost, literally) the Bellingham Young Life area director's wife, I couldn't believe it! Since the lobby was full of people, only the Lord could have orchestrated that meeting. What a blessing. I was sure she could see I was close to tears. She gave me her room key so I could deposit my things and have a nap while the attendants at the desk got things straightened out. When they called me back to the front desk, they gave me a suite on the 24th floor. The 24th floor was called the Gold floor- it had a lounge, with a continental breakfast and drinks, and pastries and snacks were served throughout the day, and into the evening. Even though I was nervous being on the 24th floor, I thanked the Lord for being so good to me.

The meetings were scheduled every few hours throughout the day, and into the evening. It was difficult going as a single person, but good for me to see how it felt to be someone on their own. I usually sat in the back of the room when I went to public meetings, but that day I decided I would be brave and sit closer to the front. I could not believe I had trouble finding a seat. People were saving three or four seats at a time. Over, and over, I heard "No sorry, These seats are saved." Feeling more lonely than ever, I finally went to the back of the room. I did not realize how vulnerable I felt being a newly single person. I thought maybe you get used to being single and alone, but I was not yet that far along in my single life. It was risky to ask permission to sit with people, and the more 'no's I got, the more rejected I felt.

I realized in the past, I had probably been guilty of doing the same thing myself - saving seats, and not knowing, or thinking of how that would make a person feel who is alone. I found myself feeling isolated, even though there were hundreds of people around. The whole trip had been quite an experience and opened my eyes to the single's world. Even though it had been uncomfortable, at times I could see I had grown through the experience, and was thankful I went to the Young Life Conference.

On the way home, I continued to be courageous, and took a small plane to Yuma to spend a few days with my sister, Jacquie, and her husband Ian. Since I had been indoors attending meetings at the conference, it felt good to be outdoors in the Arizona sunshine. I was with my sister and her husband on January 14th, which was the first anniversary of Bob's death. They had invited company over for dinner so that helped keep my mind on something other than remembering the sad day when Bob died. I arrived home the next evening. It had been a good trip, but I was glad to be home.

During this trip I realized there comes a time in our lives when we have to push ourselves out of our comfort zone, in order to grow. We may need to do some things we are fearful of, and as we take one step, then another, we are building our faith and trust that the Lord walks right along with us. It is a wonderful feeling of accomplishment, to conquer our fears!!

CHAPTER 27

In February, I had several weeks of feeling totally alone, anxious and unmotivated. One of my friends suggested I might be depressed. I thought the way I was feeling was just part of the grieving process. I knew the Lord was with me, and I was grateful for that, but I was still feeling lonely and I wondered if I should try working again. During this time, several job opportunities began to present themselves. Formerly, I had taken a class at the Joanne Wallace institute on Image Improvement so I decided to give an Image Improvement class for teenage girls.

The class covered several topics, including, dating, etiquette, manners, how to set a nice table for special dinners, how to get in and out of a car gracefully, color analysis and how to dress appropriately. For one class, I arranged for a hair stylist to come and demonstrate hair styles that were right for each girl's facial shape. For the wardrobe class, Nordstrom's provided clothing for the girls to try on, determining which styles complemented their body types. The class was called 'Beauty from the Inside Out', and was taught from a Christian perspective. The course lasted six weeks. The girls, and their moms, loved the class, and I enjoyed teaching it.

Shortly after the class was over, I got a job as a receptionist at a beauty salon. I enjoyed that but felt I was just going through the motions. I realized this was not something I wanted to do for the rest of my life. I also began taking a night class once a week in Burnaby, for counseling training. My friend, who worked at a local TV station, called and said they were looking for a makeup artist for their commercials, and would I be interested? I accepted the position. It became a challenge, when the cameraman said that he wanted people to look like a ripe peach, so the camera would pick up their color. This meant I needed to apply the makeup heavier than usual. I enjoyed my time as a makeup artist at the TV station. I was on call for about six weeks before I revisited my calling towards Christian counseling.

February 14th was my second Valentine's Day without Bob. I could feel myself slipping into the old routine of self pity again. It seemed everywhere I looked, there were flowers and heart shaped chocolates. I missed Bob and all the special things he used to do for me on holidays. I cried most of the afternoon, before going to dinner with a friend. While I was away at dinner, the children called and left messages and that made me feel better.

One evening in March, as I watched a sad movie I realized Bob was becoming more distant to me, and I began to cry. It had been fourteen months since he died, and I was no longer able to feel his presence, or the comfort of his memory. I could see I was not thinking of him as often, and had a harder time bringing his face up in my mind. Now, I realized I was adapting to being alone. There was a healing, and 'letting go' taking place. I did not want to let go, but I knew I must. It was time to move on.

CHAPTER 28

One day that summer, my daughter Patti went to Stanley Park to sit on her dad's bench. When she got there, a man from Italy was sitting on the bench. She visited with him and he told her his Visa was running out and he did not know if he should renew it or go back home. He shared with her how he felt lonely, and that after reading the plaque on the back of the bench, he began to talk to Bob about what was going on in his life. He said he felt Bob's presence, and that a peace came over him. He was no longer anxious about the decision he had to make.

One time when I visited Bob's bench, there was a young man in his twenties sitting on it. As I visited with him, I told him that it was my husband's bench. He said he came often and sat there and talked with Bob about problems he was going through, and decisions he had to make. He felt as if he were talking to his father, and that he felt Bob's presence. He shared with me how he loved coming to Bob's bench, and what a special man he must have been. My heart was warmed to hear those words. I wondered how many others had been helped by sitting on Bob's bench. I hoped Bob would know how God was using him to help others, and how much that knowledge comforted me.

Early in October, 1990, my sister Jean called, and told me that my dad had a massive stroke, and I should come to the hospital. I prayed all the way there, but by the time I got arrived he was gone. I was in shock. It was sad to see my mom sitting in the waiting room looking so small, like she was in shock herself. She had that look of numbness about her that I knew so well. My sisters and I stayed with her awhile, to comfort her.

The following October, 1991, I was on a short- term mission trip working at an orphanage in Mexico, when my sister called and told me mom was in the hospital in serious condition, with a heart attack. I caught the next flight home, praying all the way, and hoping I could see her before she passed away. When I landed at the airport, I got the news that she had died a few hours before I arrived. Both my parents were eighty-two years old when they died. That made three major deaths for me in a three year period. I went through a lot of grieving during those years. Death is a normal part of our life journey and something we all have to face. The Lord was close to me during that time, giving me comfort.

CHAPTER 29

Almost two years after Bob's death, my friend introduced me to a very nice man named Pete, who had lost his wife some time earlier. My doctor had been encouraging me to start dating, so I met with Pete, and discovered that he was a Christian, liked to play golf, dance, and go for walks. Since I enjoyed all those things, we had a lot in common.

The first few months, we went for walks, had coffee and enjoyed many dinner dates. For some reason, the first Sunday he accompanied me to church, I felt sad. I had been used to either being alone, or having Bob sitting next to me. Now it was hard to be sitting in church with another man beside me, but I realized I had to let go of Bob and make a new life for myself. I cried most of that Sunday afternoon. I felt scared, and sad, to begin this new phase of my life.

I planned a short term mission trip to an orphanage in Mexico in April 1991, Pete said he wanted to go along. We went with a church group from Delta, B.C., and as they passed through Bellingham they picked us up on their way. We stayed overnight at several different churches along the way. It was a fantastic experience. I signed up to serve at the orphanage for three more months, from September through November that year. I still was not sure what God wanted me to do with my life, so I thought this would be a good test to see if he wanted me to be a missionary.

Pete and I got to know each other well on that trip. That summer, we talked about getting married. He was such a nice man and we had so much in common, it seemed right. But by the fall, every time I thought of marrying him, I was flooded with feelings of disappointment. These feelings were so strange, I felt it must not be what God wanted for me. We decided to just be friends and see what developed. While I was away at the orphanage for those three months, Pete met someone else, and they married. A part of me was relieved, and I was happy for him. But it was hard to be alone again.

Before I left for the mission trip, I had gone for an interview at Burden Bearers counseling office in Langley, B.C. They told me to come back after my mission trip and there would be a place for me in their office when I returned. That spring, I began training to become a counselor at Burden Bearers Counseling Ministries. I had to be supervised for 500 hours before I was allowed to see clients on my own. I loved the work, and felt I was where God wanted me to be.

Now that Pete was married, there were times I felt overwhelmed by loneliness. I remember walking to the mailbox to collect my mail, feeling the sadness of being alone. In my mailbox, there was a newsletter from Burden

Bearers, and in it was an article called 'Believe and be Satisfied', written by St. Anthony of Padua in the 12th century.

It read; Dear Child,
"Everyone longs to give themselves completely to someone,
To have a deep soul relationship with another
To be loved thoroughly and exclusively.
But to the Christian, God says, "No, not until you are satisfied,
Fulfilled and content with being loved by me alone,
With giving yourself totally and unreservedly to me.
With having an intensely and unique relationship with me alone.
Discovering that only in me is your satisfaction to be found,
Will you be capable of the perfect human relationship
That I have planned for you.
You will never be united to another
Until you are united with me.
Exclusive of anyone or anything else.
Exclusive of any other desires or longings.
I want you to stop planning, to stop wishing, and allow me to give you
The most thrilling plan existing - one you cannot imagine.
I want you to have the best.
Please allow me to bring it to you.
You must keep watching me, expecting the greatest things.

Keep experiencing the satisfaction that I am.
Keep listening, and learning the things that I tell you.
Just wait, that's all.
Don't be anxious, don't worry
Don't look around at the things others have gotten
Or that I have given them
Don't look around at the things you think you want,
Just keep looking off and away; up to me,
Or you will miss what I want to show you.
And then when you are ready, I'll surprise you with a love
Far more wonderful than you could dream of.
You see, until you are ready and until the one I have for you is ready,
I am working even at this moment
To have you both ready at the same time.
Until you are both satisfied exclusively with me,
And the life I have prepared for you,
You won't be able to experience the love that exemplifies your
relationship with me.
And this is perfect love.
And dear one, I want you to have this most wonderful love.
I want you to see in the flesh a picture of your relationship with me.
And to enjoy in the flesh a picture of your relationship with me.
And to enjoy materially and concretely, the everlasting union

Of beauty, perfection and love that I offer you with myself.

Know that I love you utterly. For I am God. Believe it and be satisfied."

As I read this article in the newsletter, my spirit soared. I agreed we all want a deeply personal and intimate relationship with another. Someone who knows our heart, the good and bad thoughts we have but loves us anyway. God wants to be that person in our lives. When we put Him first then we are ready to love another like He loves us. I felt the poem was saying to me, when the time is right someone will come into my life but God needs to fill me up and be first and foremost in my life. My hope was restored as I felt like God was impressing on me that one day, when I was ready I would have a husband again.

At the writing of this book, the Lord has not brought that person into my life as yet, but I am trusting that if it is the Lord's will and I have not misinterpreted the message, that day will come. I am beginning to realize that I may have mistaken the message as a promise when instead it was meant to encourage me and give me hope, which it did at that difficult time in my life.

CHAPTER 30

About five years after Bob died, my daughter-in-law Janelle, came to me and said her church was having a class on grieving. She encouraged me to attend. I did not see it as something I needed, as I thought I was doing well, but after praying for a few days, I decided to take her advice. I discovered it was one of the best things I could have done. I began to see there were a lot of unresolved issues deep inside me that I needed to address.

The name of the class was, "Death, Dying and Mourning, Schedule of Letters." Each week we wrote a letter, on a suggested topic, and then shared it with each other in the class the next time we met. It was very painful, but a tremendous help in the healing process. I was shocked at all the emotion that was inside me. I was not aware I was still stuck in my grief and needed to move forward. I share the following, unedited letters I wrote at that time, not to belittle my husband in any way, but to show how easy it is to be stuck in grief, and not be able to move on, especially when there are unresolved issues in the marriage. The emotions that I share in the following letters were from my point of view, mostly from the first ten years of our marriage. It shocked me to see how long I had been hanging on to these deeply buried emotions.

The following are actual letters from our grieving class in 1994.

1994, LETTER # 1:
LETTER OF GRIEF

At class last week, I kept feeling like I was going to cry. What is that all about Lord? What is going on? I am glad Bob is with you, and is out of pain now. He is at peace and rest in his soul, he is happy. I feel I have grieved well. I have read all the books I could find on grieving and how to do it. I have allowed myself to cry my eyes out, when I needed to. I would take any day I needed to cry, and have a pity party. I miss him so much sometimes, yet I would not want him back. I am so angry, I can feel it way down deep inside me. Our relationship was so painful sometimes; mostly in the first ten years. I hated you Bob, you hurt me so much. You shut me out of your life. I was so needy, I needed you to love me. I felt used and unloved. You were more interested in your friends and being out drinking with them, than being a husband and a father. You were so irresponsible, yet you could charm the socks off me. The only thing you took responsibility for was our financial affairs. You paid the bills and always provided for us that way, but you never let me have any money beyond the grocery fund, which was minimal. I felt like I was nothing to you. Anything I ever asked of you, you said that I didn't need it, my needs didn't matter. How could I have been so

154

stupid? How could I let you treat me that way? People were always giving us boxes of clothing for the kids, and for me. I was grateful for that, but to this day I wonder why we always had to wear other people's things. You would complain about having to buy socks and underwear when the kids needed them. How dare you treat us like that! How dare you pull into yourself and not talk to me. I would yell and scream at you like an idiot and you would not even respond. Do you know how frustrating that was? I hated you and yet I loved you so much. You could make my heart melt and I would do anything for you. You knew that. How many times I wanted to leave but where could I go with four little kids? The times I did leave, after a day or so, I missed you so much I had to come back. How painful! You did whatever you wanted and because I didn't drive I felt I was stuck at home taking care of the kids. I hate you for robbing me of the joy of raising my kids. I hated the responsibility. I was scared to death staying home by myself with them until two or three am while you were out drinking. What if something happened to them? I was home all the time and could not go anywhere as I did not drive. You had me right where you wanted me. You controlled me. You never had the guts to stand up to me, you just let me rant on and on, and would shut yourself off. You did exactly what you wanted, and I never had any say in it. I was trying so hard to get the love I needed from you that I had none to give my kids. I was shutting them out just as you were doing to me. I loved them so much but they were very demanding. It was tough raising four children under six years old by myself. Someone was always needing me. I know now, they were as needy as I was. How sad that neither of us could give them the love they needed, or deserved, and they suffered for it.

1994, LETTER # 2:
DESCRIPTION OF GRIEF AND ATTITUDES
TOWARDS DEATH AND DYING

After the first shock of finding out the cancer was terminal, I settled into numbness. Especially the first few months, visiting Seattle for second opinions, standing by while Bob was trying to decide whether or not to take treatment. I remember driving home from Seattle after the doctor told him he had one to two years, maybe less. I felt in a daze. We talked about our feelings, what I would do, and what my future would look like on my own. I remember feeling very close to Bob. I felt like it was the first time we had ever had a deep conversation, where he let me in to what he was thinking. I remember him saying he was scared of pain. The doctor assured him they could control the pain. Bob said if they could, then dying would be a piece of cake.

I tried so hard to back off and let him make the decision himself about taking chemo therapy. I was always a 'take charge' type of person; quick to give my opinions, and take control. Unfortunately, Bob had let me do that and I had been trying hard the last few years to let him take the lead, even though he really didn't want to. I felt like the decision for chemo therapy was his. It was his life, and up to him how he chose to live the rest of it. Bob decided not to take any treatment. Part of me was glad because he was feeling so good physically at the time and I did not want to see that change, but part of me was also scared. What if he was shortening his life by not taking any treatment?

I remember us going to the health food store in Bellingham. The owner had overcome cancer in his life so we came out loaded up with all kinds of liver cleansing products. It made Bob have dark circles under his eyes, and he said he resembled a skunk. That lasted about a week, and then Bob said that was enough. He would rather die than go out of the house looking like that, but he did continue taking the mega vitamins.

I remember driving home from work one day, feeling like a dark cloud was coming down on me and smothering me. It was so heavy, I felt like I was being crushed. I ran into the house and lay across the bed and the floodgates opened as I let the tears flow. I was completely overwhelmed with pain, I cried and cried, and finally this devastating cloud lifted. That was one of my darkest times. Bob and I spent a lot of time talking, and sharing about our feelings. It was a wonderful time because this had never happened before in our marriage. Before, I always felt like he shut me out and didn't need me. Now he did need me and it felt good. We both became very close to God and to each other. We read Billy Graham's book, Facing Death, and another little one called 'Within Heaven's Gates'. These books were so good, and ministered to both Bob and I - I felt like I could hardly wait to go there. We talked a lot about Heaven, and what it would be like; not that we came to any informed conclusions.

Bob had accepted Christ a few years earlier, but was always very private about his faith. The last four years of his life, he never missed a day without reading his Bible. I read everything I could find on death and dying, and grieving and widowhood, so I could be prepared for losing Bob. We had a hospital bed at home in October, and he died in January. As Bob had slipped into a coma those last few days together were extremely difficult, but the Lord's presence was so close to me I felt lifted above what was going on around me, and the Lord carried me through it. I had the privilege of holding Bob's hand as he took his last breath. It was a wonderful experience, knowing he had left us and was in the presence of God. There is a verse in 11 Corinthians that says "To be absent from the body is to be present with the Lord"

1994, LETTER # 3:
DESCRIPTION OF THE LOVED ONE WHO DIED

Bob was an only child. His mom was divorced when he was two years old and remarried when he was eight. Bob fought with his mother a lot trying to come to grips with his hurts. He was sent to live with his birth dad when he was fifteen yrs old. He was a troubled teenager and left home when he was seventeen years old. He got room and board at various places and lived with friends. He worked at the B.C. liquor store, drank, and partied a lot. He was conscientious, hard working, and responsible at his job. He was extremely capable and had so much potential, but never saw himself that way. He was Parts Manager for a Chevrolet dealership for ten years and the 'Reps' that came in always said his department was the best run, and most organized Parts Department in all of Washington State.

Bob's private life, was a different matter. He was

irresponsible, and would not follow through on commitments or promises. He would not come home after work three or four nights a week, and then would try to charm his way back in, saying, "I am sorry, I will never do it again." I would fall for it. He was fun – loving, and could make me laugh. I loved being with him, for the first few years, anyway; most of the time. As we began to fight, he would tell me everything was my fault. It was all in my head. He loved to flirt. He would pick out one person in our lives and concentrate on them for awhile, until I had had enough. Then we wouldn't see them for awhile and he would start in on someone else. He always said I was nuts, or jealous, and I was constantly trying to figure out if it was him or me. I used to think if he would only stop drinking, that behavior would stop too. I used to think he had a magnetic personality, as the women would gravitate towards him and he would respond. How naïve. Years later, after I started getting healthier myself, I realized he was sending out vibes. As soon as we were out with people, he would immediately shut me out emotionally. It was like I was not there. He would make jokes about me that were put downs, relating some of the dumb things I would do, and we would all laugh. He would be the life of the party, at my expense. I would watch him go into a room and scout it out for potential flirting partners. I would feel completely abandoned. When he got Cancer and quit drinking, I thought the flirting would stop then but it didn't. I realized he had a definite problem. It was an addiction with him. When I confronted him about it, he said, "I don't know how I get myself into these things."

I remember the children wanted to give us a 25th

anniversary party, and I said, no. I didn't want all his drinking buddies sharing painful memories from the past that they thought were funny, but were so hurtful to me. The kids rented a limousine and took us to dinner instead, which was wonderful. As Bob was dying, I realized how sensitive he really was. He let me see glimpses of himself, now and again. He said whenever he had a problem throughout his life, he would have a drink and forget about it. He asked me one day, "Do you think I was an alcoholic?" I remember the shock on his face when the realization hit him that he was. I didn't need to say anything. He became very needy, and as time went on I loved him as I would a child. I felt like his mother all through our marriage and at the end of his life he drew from me for his comfort and strength.

I have no doubt he loved me in his own way. I have no idea what it would be like to be loved by a man in a healthy way. Both my father, and my husband were unhealthy relationships for whatever reason. I used to ask God to bring a man into my life who would really love me but that is not important anymore. I have learned how much God loves me and that is enough for me. I am so grateful for Bob, and for the years we had together. He made me what I am today and I like that person. I didn't like who I used to be. God put us together, and He doesn't make mistakes.

1994, LETTER # 4:
LETTER OF GOODBYE

Dear Bob,

I need to write this letter saying goodbye to you. Why is

that so hard for me? I have struggled with this all week. I think if I put it down on paper, you will be gone and I don't want that. I don't want to let go. Why is that? It's not that I always felt secure being married to you. I didn't. But part of me did. I liked the security of being married. I don't like being alone. I feel like if I let go of you, I will be floundering around down here by myself. I have always been afraid to be alone. Yet, I am not really alone, God is with me. He has always been there, even before I knew Him, and since you have been gone, He answers me before I even ask. I know there is no one that could take care of me the way God does, so why am I afraid to trust Him? I feel like if I let go of you, it will be like stepping off a cliff, waiting for God to catch me before I fall.

I really appreciate and am glad for the time we had together Bob. The first ten years were dreadful, but I know I was a good part of that too. I came into the marriage with so much anger at my dad and I took it out on you. I know now that it must have been hard living with me. I can thank you for being so hard, and unbending, because I got to the end of myself, and found the Lord. I may never have done that if I could have changed you, as I tried to do. I loved you with every part of my being. That is why it hurt so much.

I experienced many different kinds of love for you as we went through the stages of our life together. You always provided for me, financially. I never had to worry about the bills not being paid. I appreciate that. I love you for the way you got everything in order before you died, right down to supplying me with all the parts I would need for tune-ups, for my car for several years. I loved your sense of humor. That is what got us through the rough times. I remember when we were making funeral arrangements, how we couldn't agree on what we wanted on our headstone. You wanted Fir trees, and I wanted scripture and praying hands. I remember feeling the tension, but neither of us would back down. It was important to both of us. It was important to me because it would be my headstone too, one day. It was so funny, and we both laughed, that even to our dying day we couldn't agree, but in the end we compromised. The fir trees are above your name and the praying hands above mine, with the scripture along the bottom.

The best memory I have of you is when you were dying. You hadn't spoken for several days and you mustered up all your strength and tried to pull yourself up, looked me square in the eye and said, "I love you, baby." You never spoke again. That meant so much to me and always will. The night you died, I went to bed at 11:30 pm, on the floor beside your bed. I woke up at 12:30 am, with a start. I heard you breathing so I took your hand and held it, and told you I loved you. You let out this long gentle sigh, and then you were gone. I hope you know I was there with you.

The Lord was so gracious. After all we had been through together, He let me be there as He took you home. I am glad you are home with Him. I know life was hard for you at times. You were so bound up and worried about what people thought of you, you weren't free here. You are free now, and I am glad. So I will say goodbye now, as hard as that is. You were part of my life for thirty years and I learned many things from you. I love you and will never forget you, dear Bob

1994 LETTER # 5:
HOW I WILL REMEMBER BOB

Dear Bob,

I will always remember the first time I met you. You had a smile that made my knees go weak. I remember thinking,' he sure is cute but he's way too young for me,' of course, I found out later, you were six years older than I was. I loved the happy -go -lucky way about you. You loved to have fun, even though that was hard to live with over the years. I want to remember you for that, without the pain involved. I loved your sense of humor. We had so many good laughs together. I loved how we could look at each other across the room and know we were both thinking the same thing, and have a good laugh about it. You had such a sweet, gentle spirit.

I remember your mom's friend saying you had an angelic look about you. Everyone loved you. You were always the life of the party, in your quiet way. People were drawn to you. I remember you for your neatness. You were so organized and meticulous. I remember all the special times we had walking around Stanley Park. You would hold my hand, or put your arm around my waist as we walked. How special that was for me. You began to share yourself with me, and talk about life and death. I saw how sensitive you were. I love to remember what a good dancer you were. We had some wonderful times together. You added a dimension of fun to my life. I think I will remember you most for your sense of humor.

1994, LETTER # 6:
LETTER OF CONSOLATION

Dear Lord,

How good you are to me. How wonderful is your care for me. You said in your word you would be a husband to me. You have been so much more. You take care of every detail of my life, from big things to small things. You know my every thought. So many times I have not even needed to ask for something, I just thought about it and it was done. You have gone ahead of me every step of the way. You have encouraged me to step out and face my fears. I think of my first trip by myself, one year after Bob died. I met Pam on that flight. We enjoyed each other so much that we stayed friends for a long time. There was a mix up with the hotel reservation and I was sent down the hall to a large room to wait. There were 2400 people registered for that Young Life Convention, and they didn't think they would have a room for me. As I walked down the hall I was ready to lose it, when I met the Young Life area director's wife from Bellingham, walking toward me. She gave me the key to their room so I could go there to rest. When I went back later to the registration desk, they gave me a room on the "gold floor", they called it. It was on the 26th floor. Lord you know my fear of heights and fires in hotels but I had to take it. You gently led me into situations to enable me to grow through my fears.

Freeway driving has always been a big fear of mine. I pray every time I have to get on the freeway and you always seem to clear a path for the onramp, holding back the traffic until I get on.

When I felt you leading me into counseling, you opened wide the doors for training opportunities. You gave me the courage to drive to Canada, and provided me with friends to stay with when I needed to be there. You provided the perfect job for me at Burden Bearers. You provide for me financially, when I didn't know where the money was coming from to pay my bills.

You provided me with my Mexico mission trip before I started working there so I would get to the end of myself and depend on you and not on my own strength and knowledge. I know that apart from you, I can do nothing. I praise you for loving me so much, and being so patient with me. My whole life, I have been afraid of so many things. You are helping me to face those fears and I love you for it. I do not want to be crippled by fear any longer. The day after Bob died, when I was getting ready to go to the funeral home, I remember hearing something and I realized I was singing, "Count Your Blessings." You moved right in, and I felt your presence so close to me. I felt like we were one. I was glad Bob was with you, and free at last from all that bound him. I remember thinking, "Now it's just you and me Lord, I am giving my life over to you, again. I want you to use me in whatever way you want. I know you want me to be free of all that binds me, as well. Thank you for your loving kindness to me. I think of the verse you gave me when I first became a Christian. Philipians 4:13 NAS, "I can do all things through Him who strengthens me." I know whatever you ask of me, you will enable me to do it. My heart aches with love for you, and it is my prayer I will not lose that."

I will be ever grateful to my daughter-in-law Janelle,

for encouraging me to attend that grief class. As hard as it was, writing those letters and sharing them out loud in the group helped me to release the hurt and anger I was holding deep within me, and to move on from being stuck in my grief. I realized I was walking the same path Bob and his mother had walked, having unresolved issues. I should have talked through those issues when Bob gave a general apology earlier, no matter how much it would have hurt Bob and I. I now believe it may have brought us even closer, but instead I gave into the fear that it would hurt too much.

After the class was over, I was released to love Bob with forgiveness in my heart, realizing that his behavior those first years of our marriage was because of hurts in his life that he had not dealt with. Writing those letters helped me to let go and move on. Grieving is an ongoing process, different for each individual, and I wonder if we are ever completely finished? But, as time goes on, the memories become sweet and less painful. I would recommend to anyone grieving, writing letters as I did in the class to the person who died is one of the best ways to release the pain and be able to move forward.

Eight years after Bob's death, I felt the desire to move. I had lived in our condo for so many years, I began to miss not being able to step out into a yard. I found property at Birch Bay, Washington. It was two-thirds of an acre with a beautiful large cedar tree, shaped like a Christmas tree, right in the middle of the property. As soon as I saw the tree I knew that was my property. I loved that tree, and planned the landscaping around it, making a fire pit close by so I could sit there in the evenings enjoying my surroundings.

I hired a contractor to help clear the land and prepare it for my new home. One evening, I was sitting at the fire pit with a friend and he suggested I remove the bottom limbs of the tree. I said, "Oh No!" I loved the way the branches swept so beautifully onto the ground, making it look so majestic. There was one branch on the bottom that was dead, so he suggested taking it off and I agreed, grateful for his help. When I came home from an outing a few days later, I was shocked as I looked at my cedar tree. My friend had come while I was gone and cut away almost one third of the lower branches, I could not believe my eyes. I was devastated and felt violated, and strangely embarrassed, for my beautiful tree. It looked so bare, and naked. I called my friend and left a message telling him how hurt and angry I was that he would come and strip the tree after I had given him permission to take only one branch off at the bottom.

As the days went on I kept looking out my window at my tree, now so naked and bare. My thoughts went to Jesus, and how He must have felt hanging on the cross, stripped almost naked, and severely beaten. He said, "Father, forgive them, for they know not what they do." I knew I would have to forgive my friend if I was to have peace, or it would continue to hurt me. As I gazed out over the yard, the thought came to me about writing a children's story about the tree and forgiveness. I had never thought of myself as a writer, but the more I looked at my tree the more the story unfolded. I wrote a children's book called "The Tree of Forgiveness", in 1998, and dedicated it to my grandchildren. It was exciting to see how God could take what I thought was such a tragedy and make something positive out of it.

CHAPTER 31

After much thought and prayer, in 2003 I moved from Birch Bay, Washington back to British Columbia. I had grown up at Pender Harbour, B.C., on the Sunshine Coast, and felt very strongly, that was the area to which I should move. When I was growing up, there were no churches in Pender Harbour, so after becoming a Christian many years later, I frequently prayed for the Sunshine Coast. I went for a weekend visit and found there were many churches now, and that they had prayer meetings once a month, where several churches came together to pray for unity and revival. Since my heart was to pray for the area, I moved back to become a part of the prayer group but shortly after I returned, the prayer meetings stopped.

I felt the Lord wanted me to continue praying, so I started a small prayer group in my home, and we prayed together once a week. I knew there were groups of people praying all over the coast but felt sad that the large group prayer sessions, bringing folks from different churches had been disbanded. I also felt the Lord impressing upon me to write a book called "Prayers for the Sunshine Coast" and after working on it for three years, it was in print. I took my book to many pastors, and it was well received. Some pastors wanted copies to use in their Wednesday night prayer meetings. The book became popular with the local people as well.

Well, I became a widow, just as the words I heard so long ago said I would. In caring for Bob throughout his illness, I learned what it meant to truly love someone unconditionally, expecting nothing in return just as Christ loves us. As hard as it was to watch Bob deteriorating and slipping away, God was teaching me what real love meant. It was an experience I would not have asked for but counted myself as privileged to be a part of, and would not have traded for anything. 1 Corinthians 13: 4-8 NIV says, "Love is patient, love is kind. It does not envy, it does not boast, it is not proud. It is not rude, it is not self seeking, it is not easily angered, it keeps no record of wrongs. Love does not delight in evil but rejoices with truth. It always protects, always trusts, always hopes, always perseveres. Love never fails."

My journey has been long, but God has been faithful throughout, and I praise Him for my tomorrows, wherever He leads me. My desire is to serve God, and I pray that I will continue to do so as long as I am able. As I am getting older I see that if I am not able to do anything else, I can always pray. From the time many years ago, when I first became a Christian I felt like prayer has been God's calling on my life. So it is exciting for me to know I can always be used by God, maybe even more, as I get older.

He leads me to pray for my children and grandchildren, my extended family, my friends, my church, my community, and leaders of our Nations, Canada and the United States. Life is exciting, as I walk with the Lord and I look forward to each new day.

At the writing of this book, I am seventy-five years old, and have just moved into a lovely apartment building for those fifty-five and over, in the White Rock area. It is perfect for me, as there is always someone around to visit if I so desire and I can always go to my apartment if I want to be alone. I am still single, as the Lord has not brought that 'right person' into my life. I realize I have never, until now, enjoyed being single. Part of that poem I got so long ago said that God wants me to be completely His, and I realized I was looking for the man He would bring into my life, and that took over a place in my heart that should have been the Lord's. I concentrated so hard on what I thought God had promised, that I was not content. I am glad He helped me to realize the truth, and that He has blessed me with a lovely place to spend the rest of my years.

I can honestly say I am content to be single now, and feel so blessed. Yes, I am a Widow! Those words of so long ago have come to pass, but I feel like the words of Job 42: 12, are true for me, as well. Job 42: 12 NIV, " The Lord blessed the latter part of Job's life more than the first". I am loving this stage of life, and have lots of time to spend with the Lord in prayer and I believe that is what He wants me to do.

Even though my family are all traveling their own journey with the Lord, my four children and their spouses and my seven grandchildren, are all Christians. I am so

Patricia McQuarrie

proud of them and could not ask for anything more. I know I will never see Bob again this side of Heaven, but am assured we will meet again, and to that I look forward! I AM SO BLESSED !! LIFE IS GOOD!!